Praise for *Closing the Service Gap*

'This important book provides lessons for all of us on how businesses can better interact with consumers to advance economic prosperity for all.'

Dorie Clark, *Wall Street Journal* contributor; bestselling author of *The Long Game, Entrepreneurial You, Reinventing You* and *Stand Out*, which was named the #1 Leadership Book of the Year by *Inc.* magazine

'The challenge of leading an organisation while creating sustainable businesses that create economic prosperity and achieve societal good is one that few businesses can conquer. *Closing The Service Gap* pushes readers to reconsider traditional management models and power structures in the name of the engagement model of tomorrow, which will be key as businesses navigate a hybrid, post-pandemic world. A must-read for anyone taking on these challenges with customers and employees.'

Courtney Rose, Vice President at Google

'The world as a whole and, even more, the business world is learning how to re-adapt post pandemic, with the importance of understanding the whole value chain of customers-employees-organisations and how they are interconnected... Organisations, managers and employees who will fail to understand the roles of engagement and the importance of interconnections will fail to emerge on the other side of these world challenges. This book is a good starting point to understand this important lesson and build a new engagement blueprint around it.'

Tzahi Weisfeld, Vice President at Intel Corporation

'*Closing The Service Gap* provides a worthy reflection on the advancement of economic prosperity — promoting a fundamental reconsideration regarding how businesses interact with consumers. The subsequent lessons for law and policymakers, as articulated by the authors, are sizeable.'

Prachi Mathur, Business Planning and Strategy Lead EMEA at Apple

'In a world where customer obsession is an often used phrase in business, this book challenges traditional corporate principles and provides alternative, applicable suggestions on how leaders should re-think their organisation, employee and customer ecosystem. Through real life case studies, the authors' insights into organisation's application of technology are particularly relevant in succeeding in the hybrid working world we now live in.'

Dilip Mailvaganam, Senior Director at Microsoft

'*Closing The Service Gap* provides an illuminating reflection on how organisations can advance in an increasingly unpredictable and disconnected world. By fundamentally reconsidering the way companies should interact with consumers and employees, it pushes past well-meaning platitudes about balancing profit and social good to reveal a roadmap for producing both. The lessons for leaders are sizeable.'

Tasha Eurich, *New York Times* bestselling author of *Insight* and *Bankable Leadership*

'*Closing the Service Gap* is an exciting guide full of important information for those of us who want to include the client in the organisation's ecosystem. In simple language the authors share how organisations ignore the inextricable link between well-being of a company and a customer retention. This book is a roadmap to deepen the connections between customers, employees and organizational structure.'

Tatiana Mitrova, Research Fellow at the Center on Global Energy Policy at Columbia University

'*Closing the Service Gap* explains what "The customer is king" means when customers can change what they buy, and who they buy it from, at the click of a button. Employees and customers need to connect – with each other, with the firm, with its purpose and rationale – if the firm is going to produce what people want to buy, and thus be successful.'

Tim Leunig, Associate Professor at the London School of Economics

'*Closing The Service Gap* offers organisations a solution to transform and redefine their relationships with employees and customers with a fresh and actionable alternative to fatigued models of "customer obsession" that is better suited for the future of work. In a world where technology is rapidly removing boundaries and hierarchies, business innovation and success require service models that embrace connectedness and value all key players in the ecosystem equally.'

Kate Nowak, Principal Applied Scientist at Microsoft

Closing the Service Gap

Pearson

At Pearson, we believe in learning – all kinds of learning for all kinds of people. Whether it's at home, in the classroom or in the workplace, learning is the key to improving our life chances.

That's why we're working with leading authors to bring you the latest thinking and best practices, so you can get better at the things that are important to you. You can learn on the page or on the move, and with content that's always crafted to help you understand quickly and apply what you've learned.

If you want to upgrade your personal skills or accelerate your career, become a more effective leader or more powerful communicator, discover new opportunities or simply find more inspiration, we can help you make progress in your work and life.

Every day our work helps learning flourish, and wherever learning flourishes, so do people.

To learn more, please visit us at **www.pearson.com**

The Financial Times

With a worldwide network of highly respected journalists, *The Financial Times* provides global business news, insightful opinion and expert analysis of business, finance and politics. With over 500 journalists reporting from 50 countries worldwide, our in-depth coverage of international news is objectively reported and analysed from an independent, global perspective.

To find out more, visit **www.ft.com**

Closing the Service Gap

How to connect customers, employees and organisations

Benjamin Laker
Lebene Richmond Soga
Yemisi Bolade-Ogunfodun

Harlow, England • London • New York • Boston • San Francisco • Toronto • Sydney
Dubai • Singapore • Hong Kong • Tokyo • Seoul • Taipei • New Delhi
Cape Town • São Paulo • Mexico City • Madrid • Amsterdam • Munich • Paris • Milan

PEARSON EDUCATION LIMITED
KAO Two
KAO Park
Harlow CM17 9NA
United Kingdom
Tel: +44 (0)1279 623623
Web: www.pearson.com

First edition published 2023 (print and electronic)

© Pearson Education Limited 2023 (print and electronic)

The rights of Benjamin Laker, Lebene Richmond Soga and Yemisi Bolade-Ogunfodun to be identified as authors of this work have been asserted by them in accordance with the Copyright, Designs and Patents Act 1988.

The print publication is protected by copyright. Prior to any prohibited reproduction, storage in a retrieval system, distribution or transmission in any form or by any means, electronic, mechanical, recording or otherwise, permission should be obtained from the publisher or, where applicable, a licence permitting restricted copying in the United Kingdom should be obtained from the Copyright Licensing Agency Ltd, Barnard's Inn, 86 Fetter Lane, London EC4A 1EN.

The ePublication is protected by copyright and must not be copied, reproduced, transferred, distributed, leased, licensed or publicly performed or used in any way except as specifically permitted in writing by the publishers, as allowed under the terms and conditions under which it was purchased, or as strictly permitted by applicable copyright law. Any unauthorised distribution or use of this text may be a direct infringement of the authors' and the publisher's rights and those responsible may be liable in law accordingly.

All trademarks used herein are the property of their respective owners. The use of any trademark in this text does not vest in the author or publisher any trademark ownership rights in such trademarks, nor does the use of such trademarks imply any affiliation with or endorsement of this book by such owners.

Pearson Education is not responsible for the content of third-party internet sites.

ISBN: 978-1-292-44435-2 (print)
      978-1-292-44437-6 (ePub)

British Library Cataloguing-in-Publication Data
A catalogue record for the print edition is available from the British Library

Library of Congress Cataloging-in-Publication Data
Names: Laker, Ben (Benjamin), author.
Title: Closing the service gap : how to connect customers, employees and
   organisations / Benjamin Laker, Lebene Richmond Soga, Yemisi
   Bolade-Ogunfodun.
Description: First edition. | Hoboken : Pearson, 2023. | Includes
   bibliographical references and index.
Identifiers: LCCN 2023001006 | ISBN 9781292444352 (hardback) | ISBN
   9781292444369 (PDF) | ISBN 9781292444376 (ePub)
Subjects: LCSH: Organizational learning. | Customer relations.
Classification: LCC HD58.82 .L32 2023 | DDC 658.8/12—dc23/eng/20230518
LC record available at https://lccn.loc.gov/2023001006

10 9 8 7 6 5 4 3 2 1
27 26 25 24 23

Cover design by Michelle Morgan, At the Pop Ltd
Print edition typeset in 9.5/13, ITC Giovanni Std by Straive

NOTE THAT ANY PAGE CROSS-REFERENCES REFER TO THE PRINT EDITION

Contents

Acknowledgements **xi**

Publisher's acknowledgements **xiii**

About the authors **xv**

Foreword **xvii**

Introduction **xix**

Part A   Connect   **1**

    1   From empires to ecosystems   **3**

    2   Sledgehammers, optional   **25**

Part B   Strengthen   **47**

    3   There are no employees without users   **49**

    4   How to engage the distracted customer   **71**

    5   The corporate need is simple – its employees   **97**

Part C   Lead   **117**

    6   Learn to lead with RenDanHeYi   **119**

CONTENTS

7 Serve more than just the customer **143**

8 Mark the trajectory **163**

Concluding thoughts **189**

Index **195**

Pearson's Commitment to Diversity, Equity and Inclusion

Pearson is dedicated to creating bias-free content that reflects the diversity, depth and breadth of all learners' lived experiences. We embrace the many dimensions of diversity including, but not limited to, race, ethnicity, gender, sex, sexual orientation, socioeconomic status, ability, age and religious or political beliefs.

Education is a powerful force for equity and change in our world. It has the potential to deliver opportunities that improve lives and enable economic mobility. As we work with authors to create content for every product and service, we acknowledge our responsibility to demonstrate inclusivity and incorporate diverse scholarship so that everyone can achieve their potential through learning. As the world's leading learning company, we have a duty to help drive change and live up to our purpose to help more people create a better life for themselves and to create a better world.

Our ambition is to purposefully contribute to a world where:

- Everyone has an equitable and lifelong opportunity to succeed through learning.
- Our educational products and services are inclusive and represent the rich diversity of learners.
- Our educational content accurately reflects the histories and lived experiences of the learners we serve.
- Our educational content prompts deeper discussions with students and motivates them to expand their own learning and worldview.

We are also committed to providing products that are fully accessible to all learners. As per Pearson's guidelines for accessible educational Web media, we test and retest the capabilities of our products against the highest standards for every release, following the WCAG guidelines in developing new products for copyright year 2022 and beyond. You can learn more about Pearson's commitment to accessibility at:

https://www.pearson.com/us/accessibility.html

While we work hard to present unbiased, fully accessible content, we want to hear from you about any concerns or needs regarding this Pearson product so that we can investigate and address them.

- Please contact us with concerns about any potential bias at: https://www.pearson.com/report-bias.html
- For accessibility-related issues, such as using assistive technology with Pearson products, alternative text requests, or accessibility documentation, email the Pearson Disability Support team at:

    disability.support@pearson.com

Acknowledgements

We would like to extend our gratitude to RenDanHeyi Model Research Institute (HMI) for granting us access and opening the doors for our primary research. We are also grateful for the vast amounts of secondary data, reports and other materials that were made available.

Publisher's acknowledgements

10 Joseph Schumpeter: Quoted by Joseph Schumpeter; **11 Winston Churchill:** Quoted by Winston Churchill; **12 Henry Ford:** Quoted by Henry Ford; **14 Walid Negm:** Quoted by Walid Negm; **20-21 Matthew Tirrell:** Quoted by Matthew Tirrell; **42 Kevin Simzer:** Quoted by Kevin Simzer; **43 Anand Srivatsa:** Quoted by Anand Srivatsa; **55 John Law:** Quoted by John Law; **75 Peter Drucker:** Quoted by Peter Drucker; **79 David Ogilvy:** Quoted by David Ogilvy; **106 Pearson Education:** Yukl, G. A. (2006) Leadership in Organizations. Upper Saddle River: Pearson Prentice Hall; **110 Springer Nature:** Danah Zohar (2021), Zero Distance Management in the Quantum Age. Springer Nature; **111 James F. Moore:** Quoted by James F. Moore; **121 Ralph Melvin Stogdill:** Quoted by Ralph Melvin Stogdill; **146 Springer Nature:** Grint, K. (2005) Leadership: Limits and Possibilities. Basingstoke: Palgrave Macmillan; **172 University of California:** Luft, J.; Ingham, H. (1955). "The Johari window, a graphic model of interpersonal awareness". Proceedings of the Western Training Laboratory in Group Development. Los Angeles: University of California, Los Angeles; **177 Henry Mintzberg:** Quoted by Henry Mintzberg.

About the authors

Professor Benjamin Laker is a Professor of Leadership and Director of Impact and External Engagement at Henley Business School, University of Reading, who studies the impact of leadership on society. He has published research in *Harvard Business Review, Human Resource Management,* the *Journal of Consumer Research and MIT Sloan Management Review*. His previous book, the *Financial Times* bestseller Too Proud to Lead – which focused on corporate and political collapses and scandals – was praised by *The Daily Telegraph*.

Dr Lebene Richmond Soga is an Associate Professor of Management Practice and Entrepreneurship at Henley Business School, University of Reading. His research explores a range of themes, including the social aspects of digital technologies in organisational life, entrepreneurship and manager–employee relationships. He regularly presents his research at international conferences for business leaders, academics and policymakers to progress the understanding of various organisational challenges. His research insights are featured in *The Wall Street Journal, Forbes,* the *Financial Times,* ACCA Global and several other international outlets. He has published in leading journals, including *Organisational Research Methods, Small Business Economics, European Journal of Work and Organisational Psychology, Technological Forecasting and Social Change, Harvard Business Review* and *MIT Sloan Management Review,* among others.

Dr Yemisi Bolade-Ogunfodun is a Programme Director and Lecturer in Organisational Behaviour at Henley Business School, University of Reading. Her research interests take a cultural perspective of diverse organisational contexts and explore interactions in values and meaning systems, social aspects of work, as well as effects of cultural incongruence on the experience of work. She frequents international research symposia – regularly presenting her research to academics, practitioners and policymakers. She has published seminal papers in leading academic and practitioner outlets, including *Organisational Research Methods, Journal of Business Research, Harvard Business Review* and *MIT Sloan Management Review,* among others. She also frequently contributes to published volumes with major publishing houses such as Emerald Publishing and Edward Elgar Publishing.

Foreword

The platform economy has given rise to a new breed of organisation built around providing an exceptional customer experience. These organisations have re-thought every aspect of their operations to deliver a level of user experience unmatched in their respective industries. In doing so, they have disrupted entire industries by putting the customer first. In turn, this has created a new breed of customers – termed 'prosumers' by Alvin Toffler. Prosumers shape public opinion about a brand or company by consuming products or services and then writing reviews, posting photos and tweeting about their experiences. This has created a new way of doing business – the sharing economy – think Airbnb and Uber. This book is a valuable resource for anyone seeking to understand these new business models.

In the past, when an organisation wanted to understand its customers, it would commission customer surveys or focus groups. However, this process was costly and time-consuming, and the results were often unreliable. By contrast, the platform economy provides real-time feedback loops that allow businesses to understand and respond to customer needs and wants rapidly. This is the fundamental difference between the old and new economies: whereas the former was based on a linear, top-down model of production, the latter is based on a networked, bottom-up model where customers are co-creators.

This rise of the platform economy has allowed a new way of engaging with customers: a symptom of the freedom and speed of information enabled by new technologies, transforming customer engagement from *caveat emptor* to *caveat venditor*. The key to the phenomenon is its network effect – as more people join a platform and contribute, the platform becomes more valuable to everyone involved. It is this ecosystem that the authors of *Closing the Service Gap* analyse and discuss, and they have produced a must-read for anyone looking to build or grow a platform business.

In this book, the authors provide a framework for understanding the platform economy and its key players. They also offer practical advice on how to compete in this new economy. After all, if the customer is now indeed king, the race is on to get as close to them as possible and do more for them than ever before, prompting a fundamental reconsideration of how businesses interact with consumers and internal management methods enable closer customer proximity. And that requires a different kind of leader – one focused on empowering others, responding quickly to change and creating a customer service culture. *Closing the Service Gap* challenges existing thought so that a leader who wishes to leverage a new era of customer-centrism can do so with ecosystem thinking.

This book's implications for leaders – and business schools that teach leadership, such as Henley – are enormous. Consider this, for example: if the customer is now in charge, does that mean marketing is dead? And if so, what should take its place? How can leaders create a customer service culture within their organisations? What new skills and capabilities do they need to succeed in this new environment? And lastly, what does this mean for leadership development programmes? This book is a valuable resource for anyone seeking to understand these questions, among others, to prepare for the future.

One thing is certain: those who succeed in this new era will be people who think differently about the customer. I would encourage all business leaders to read it and join me in ushering in a new customer-centric era by closing the service gap. Are you up for the challenge?

Terence Mauri
Founder, Hack Future Lab, MIT Entrepreneur Mentor,
and Visiting Professor at IE Business School

Introduction

Why is this book important?

The world we face today is a complex one, yet it is one filled with opportunity for those who are brave enough to lean in, brave enough to confront the fears of what lies ahead and brave enough to not simply flex or adapt or follow in the path of others. Many may argue that the word 'ecosystem' has become over-used and has become yet another word to frame how an organisation seeks to compete, adapt or survive. The truth is that the concept of an ecosystem as an interconnected network is not over-used, far from it. It is under-used, and herein lies both the opportunity and the challenge. The opportunity lies in knowing and, equally importantly, doing something about the fact that we, as individuals, and the society and communities in which we all live and work are no longer independent of each other. They can't be, as the interconnectivity that has been built over the years has made that a fact. In traditional management of people, there was always subject and object, the manager being the subject and the managed being the object. But in the Internet of Things (IoT) era, featuring decentralisation, disintermediation and distributed leadership, everyone is the main subject of the enterprise, not staying in the context of subject and object. Employees are turned into autonomous people, organisations are transformed into microenterprises within an ecosystem, and leadership in the traditional sense now becomes shared.

The challenge, therefore, is to grasp what this means in terms of how we lead organisations and how we create sustainable businesses that create economic prosperity and achieve societal good. Can we truly move beyond rhetoric and well-meaning platitudes and deliver both? Are well-meaning intentions enough to carry us forward? It all comes down to what you do, not only what you say. Let us say you enter a restaurant to

INTRODUCTION

enjoy your favourite meal. The server comes but stands 10 metres away. 'The meal is ready,' they exclaim and say nothing more. Now, the rest is up to you. What would you do in such a situation? Isn't it the case that in a typical restaurant, you would expect to have your server stand close to you, smile and engage with you in a way that makes you feel comfortable and appreciated? Unfortunately, this metaphor of the distant server is representative of what we have observed in contemporary organisations. Indeed, there is a hierarchical distance in many organisations which is often taken as given. Traditional management models have typically emphasised the power structure in the organisation, where the boss is at the top of the hierarchy, managers are positioned below him or her and operational staff at various levels are positioned further down the hierarchy. So how does the customer fit into this structure? The customer is usually thought of as being outside the organisation. But this is not really true, is it? Without the customer, no sales can be made, no revenue comes in, no salaries can be paid and the organisation as a going concern will be under threat. So, we can agree that the customer is key to business success. However, many businesses fail despite having good products and a database of customers.

In fact, the reality in the current age of digitisation and social media is that customers can be easily distracted by the many competing products out there. Furthermore, buying is at the click of a keypad, as traditional shops are replaced by online platforms. So, really, the challenge is keeping your customer sufficiently engaged, such that they continue to give *you* repeat business. For many business leaders, this remains a black box. Much efforts and capital expenditure have gone into technology that captures customer buying habits, preferences and digital footprints on their company webpages. However, it is still a buyer's market, and all companies can do is position their products, segment the market and target their focal customer groups. Keeping customers engaged is an ongoing challenge, as many businesses know. This is especially the case as several service organisations deploy technology to reach large customer bases. Sadly, the quest to reach the customer through the instrumentality of technology has inadvertently become a search for the unreachable. As a manager, those you are there to serve are disengaged while you also remain '10 metres away'. This is what this book is all about. We dissect the problem confronting organisations as they seek to connect with their customer base. You will soon realise that the problem of the disengaged customer is often a problem about a disengaged organisation. Ignore the distance between you and your customers and they will soon walk away from you.

If you are a manager seeking to turn your organisation around in terms of service to your customers, this book is for you. Collectively, we bring together nearly 30 years of academic research in management and another collective 30 years of experience as practitioners in the finance, education and pharmaceutical industries to throw light on what we have come to understand is the key to an engaged organisation – one in which the customer, the employee and the organisation are all *interconnected*. Notice that we did not simply say 'connected' but rather 'interconnected'. To connect is from the Latin word *connectere*, a combination of *con* (meaning 'standby', 'alongside' or 'together') and *nectere* (meaning to 'bind'). It gives the idea of pulling something to bind onto another so they can be together. It may be that what is being bound onto another is some distance away, but they are bound together nonetheless. You simply must ensure that the one is securely integrated with what it is being bound to. By contrast, to *inter*connect means so much more. The idea of 'inter' makes both parties being bound together liable. In other words, it is not simply binding one thing to another, in which case one is the subject and the other the object. To interconnect is to ensure that both parties take part in such interconnection, holding each other in the 'bind' or 'tie'. The idea is not that they are brought together but that they *remain* together. In this book, we show why this is important when it comes to the customer, the organisation and the employee. We will use real examples and case studies to illustrate how this can be done. In fact, it is already being done by some organisations and the results are there for all to see. The proof is in the pudding.

To be clear, we are not proposing something esoteric. As academics who engage very closely with the world of work, we are aware that academic mumbo jumbo can sometimes cloud understanding. At the same time, our ideas must be based on academic rigour and research. What we have done in this book is to show you how you can take advantage of what we have 'discovered' in our research to achieve your own goals. To do so, we have introduced the concept of. . . , wait for it, RenDanHeYi – pronounced 'Ren - Dan - Her - Yee'. In case you are wondering, it is Chinese terminology. RenDanHeYi is a management philosophy that many in the West may not have heard of. In this book, we simplify what it is, how it is being deployed by a Fortune 500 organisation, and how you, too, can leverage its benefits for your own organisation. If there is any organisation that practises RenDanHeYi well, it is Haier, and so we were lucky to have been granted access to this vast organisation. Haier is a Fortune 500 organisation and a leading producer of consumer electronics in the world. We analysed what they do, engaged with nearly 200 managers and employees across different countries, and scoured several hundreds of pages of documents in our research into this company and some of their subsidiaries. We also dug into several materials about this Chinese philosophy of management. We are now ready to show you how you can deploy the principles we have learnt in your own journey. For simplicity, we use RDHY to stand for RenDanHeYi in this book and so you will find them used interchangeably.

How this book works

The book is divided into three parts. In Part A, we consider the state of businesses in the 2020s and present the case for the book: top-down empires will not survive in an environment where customers are fickle, supply chains are broken, competition is fierce and employees are stagnant. Instead, we propose the concept of a business as an ecosystem in which customers, employees and the organisation are deeply interconnected and highly dependent on one another. Definitions and a real-life case study underpin the importance of considering the 'business' through the lenses of these three stakeholders. This part of the book also introduces technology and cultural transformation as key to achieving success. We reveal the real story of RenDanHeYi and also introduce you to the RenDanHeYi model (the three-point triad connecting customers, employees and the organisation). We explore the opportunities and benefits of adopting RenDanHeYi and guide you on how to take a baseline measure of connections in your organisation.

In Part B, we consider the factors affecting the relationship (and friction) between customers and employees. You are introduced to the principle that employees should work to directly fulfil the needs of the customer and organisation. Similarly, customers only 'get what they want' if the right people and skill sets are employed. Thus, we explain the symbiotic nature of these two stakeholders, bringing this concept to life with numerous case studies. These case studies also provide you with the foundation for practical steps to deepen the relationship between your customers and employees with organisational structure and technology. Research findings highlight the dangers of not connecting the two groups, and so we provide tips to prompt you to start engaging with the two groups immediately. We also explore the connection between the organisation and the customer. With insights from spectacular leaders in renowned organisations, we consider the different perspectives that corporate boards and senior leaders have regarding their customers, both philosophically and in relation to data. We provide direction on the technology required to understand your customers' viewpoints, particularly in a world of customer disloyalty and competition for attention, and use real evidence to prove that customer satisfaction – not investor satisfaction – can make or break a business. We also offer reflective questions to prompt you to develop your understanding of the customer and the customer–organisation connection.

This part also considers the relationship between employees and the organisation. We begin by describing the employee according to RenDanHeYi: employees are highly sought-after powerhouses of capabilities that organisations need to employ to meet the needs of the customer. They are also more 'free' than ever – the notion of 'the company man' is finished in the fourth industrial revolution, against the backdrop of a highly competitive talent marketplace. With case studies, we consider the need for investment in employee engagement and company culture and explain how you can implement and reinforce the RenDanHeYi culture for new and existing employees. We discuss key factors such as culture and shared cognition, process, people factors and creating a psychologically safe climate for employees to engage in activities that help improve connections between employees and customers. We again offer practical tips to prompt you, irrespective of your level and functional area in your organisation, on how to start engaging the two groups immediately.

In the final part, Part C, we introduce you to your personal transformation journey – the notion of you transforming into a leader who thrives in a connected organisation. Using research, intimate interviews and top tips from leaders successfully adopting the RenDanHeYi model, we highlight the roles that leaders at every level can play in serving the three stakeholders of the model and in deepening the connections among all three to create long-lasting sustainable business growth. We encourage you to look beyond the ever-popular concept of 'servant leadership' (by which a leader's primary goal is to serve others above themselves) to another form of leadership that is more compatible with working in an interconnected ecosystem. Research provides us with a schema for the traits and skills of a leader who can realistically serve consumers, employees *and* the organisation, all without compromising on their resilience or the company's financial situation. We compare the two forms of leadership and then provide you with practical tips from successful leaders for your personal and professional development. The final points of the section offer you the opportunity to conduct an assessment of your current strengths and weaknesses, opportunities in the workspace and limitations, relationship with managers, supportive networks and personal values to help you develop a roadmap for developing as a leader. Practical features in this book include:

- Real-life case studies – we provide examples of practices in organisations in every chapter to help guide you in your own thinking.
- Reflective questions – each chapter ends with reflective questions and practical tips you can take in your practice.
- Practical exercises – you will find various practical exercises laced throughout the book that you can conduct with your team.
- Analytical tools – some of the tools provided are in diagrammatic format to help you engage with them more visually.
- A performance evaluation scorecard – we offer here a guide in a very simple scorecard which you can modify for your own context.

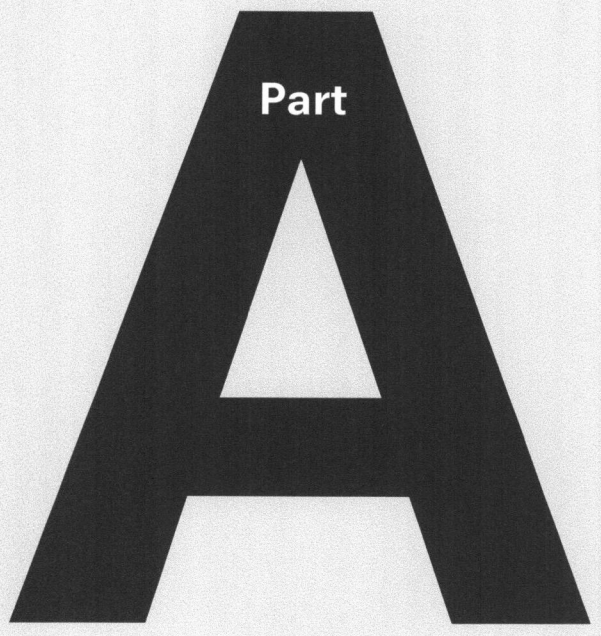

Part A

Connect

What is the state of the world of business today and how can you survive in it? Embrace the philosophy of RenDanHeYi, its principles and belief systems to transform your own organisation. It is time to find what connections you need in your business ecosystem.

From empires to ecosystems

Introduction

In this first chapter, we establish the need to reconsider the world of business. If, in the past, businesses were sheer umbrellas that protected employees from unemployment and its subsequent socioeconomic challenges, the present-day notion of what a business is looks quite different. Indeed, an employee may feel some form of economic safety but the past notions of what a business does also mean that the employee is one of the subjects of an empire that dictates how they live. In this chapter, we take a critical perspective to challenge you on how a shift in conceptualisation of a business is needed as a starting point. This is a necessary first step for change, that is, what and how we perceive reality to be. The lens from which you see the world of business will determine your approach to it. Philosophers call this your ontology, that is, your theory of reality. To position this well, we will establish in this chapter that businesses have moved from the idea of empires to what are now ecosystems.

The world of business in the twenty-first century

The twenty-first century is remarkably the most complex in terms of the variables that sustain the world of business. From the vast array of knowledge resources, made possible by the Internet, to the ever-changing technological advancements, business is not the same as it was in a world of predictability. We are living in uncertain times and this fact cannot be understated. The various advancements that humanity has witnessed (and continues to witness!) over the past two decades are not without challenges, some with devastating consequences for businesses. The 2020 COVID-19 pandemic, as an example, has intensified the challenges facing human life and business development. Under such circumstances, what most businesses urgently need now is not tinkering, but radical and disruptive transformation, born in practice, to provide soil for new theories, which in turn cultivate new practices: revolution. The dizzying rate of change in every aspect of life brought about by the third and now the fourth industrial revolution – all-encompassing social, political, environmental, technological change – is disrupting markets and changing consumer and employee attitudes and behaviour at an unprecedented rate. This is both exciting and scary, as it opens up opportunities at a faster rate than ever before, but it can also cause unexpected fallout and consequences which can be extremely challenging to navigate and react to. For example, globalisation has connected markets and economies such that capital is able to move from one part of the world to another, either creating millionaires or impoverishing investors when stock markets become volatile, which can happen in the blink of an eye.

Similarly, technological change has created alternative work models and opened up labour markets beyond the geographical borders of countries. As a result, employees can compete for jobs in any part of the world. Organisations need to embrace this pace of change, and indeed be one of the driving forces for it, but hearts and minds will always lag behind such change, and a key role, perhaps *the* key role of an organisation and its leadership, is to ensure that those hearts and minds across the organisation are informed, engaged and motivated by change, rather than threatened by it. Some aspects of these changes may mean that business leaders need to rethink how their organisations are structured. Prior to the twenty-first century, structure was everything. The manufacturing plants of the nineteenth and twentieth centuries could not function without having good 'structures' in place. This meant that, as a manager, you needed to know who was doing what, where, when, how and (arguably) why. An employee clocked in to work and it was predictable what their end of day would look like. The manager was at the helm of affairs and everything needed to be approved by him or, rarely, her. It was crystal clear who was in charge. If you didn't see the organisational chart, you felt it. If you didn't feel the hierarchy, you sensed it, and if you didn't sense it, you were doomed. It was a closely guarded empire and everyone knew where they belonged; you simply needed to work your way to the top.

The top-down hierarchical organisational structure is one that we can almost always expect to see when it comes to the design of organisations. Indeed, hierarchy has its merits - it reveals who the boss is, but also inherently shows just how far the distance is between the highest and the lowest rung of the organisational ladder. In a world of fast-paced change and expanded opportunities as a result of technology, one of the determining factors for business survival will be the ability both to anticipate and to respond to changes. What we often find is that the ways in which organisations are set up for productive work have largely remained inelastic to change. More recently, the global COVID-19 pandemic revealed the fragility in world economic systems and how vulnerable businesses are to exogenous shocks. A health crisis in one part of the world soon became a protracted global problem and economies were shut down as governments battled to contain the multifaceted threats to already delicate economies. While some businesses could no longer operate based on their existing models, others saw the need to reinvent themselves – including changing their operational structure, making radical decisions about long-held assumptions regarding in-person work and switching to remote or hybrid forms of work. Other organisations were faced with decisions about reallocation of resources away from fixed assets, such as buildings, to technology platforms that can sustain the new work model.

How about customers? Technological advancements have also created a different buying experience for customers, who now have more options than ever before. It is easier to shop around and compare prices, try out products and return them if unsatisfactory. Similarly, it is easy for customers to switch from your organisation to another. Even with everyday consumables where customers are likely to remain with the same service provider, it is now possible, at a click of a button, for households to switch allegiance, whether it be electricity, gas, water or telecommunications. Customers are also more discerning and more demanding. The rise of consumerism has meant that your customer's voice is louder than ever before. Whether you acknowledge it or not, customers have become a salient stakeholder group that cannot be ignored. In fact, they form part of the societal 'watchdog' for your organisation, evaluating your business activities through the lens of social, economic and governance principles. As an organisation, you have thus been thrust into the public eye – not only do you have to worry about keeping shareholders and investors happy, but you must also worry about the impact of wider society, where social movements have brought about changes in organisational policies regarding areas such as fairer recruitment, diversity, reward systems and accountability. The public outcry against zero-hour contracts is a prime example of how social pressure can move the hands of the clock, if only by a little.

Challenges for hierarchical operational models

From the introduction of the mechanical loom in 1784, the first industrial revolution began based on mechanised production which was later driven by steam power (see Figure 1.1). The machine was now involved in the world of work, but its role remained largely as a device that humans could use to achieve production. Managers needed to ensure that the mechanised system was operating optimally, employees were assigned specific roles, and work was a place where people spent a significant part of their day in order to meet demand or adhere to managerial control. Hierarchies were not an issue. Factories were small entities, and that form of managerial structure was a given – after all, you only had to go to 'the boss' to get issues resolved. When mass production began, with electricity now powering machines, it signalled the arrival of the second industrial revolution; notable in this era was the first conveyor belt used in a Cincinnati slaughterhouse in 1870. For work to progress at the pace of these conveyor belts, division of labour was necessary. Naturally, hierarchies emerged, as someone had to set the rules and determine who must do what. But the operational models were not so straightforward without their own challenges. Bottlenecks in factory operations soon became evident, and the division of labour almost reduced people to machines, as a worker could go to work all day with only one job to do, e.g. turn a screw to the right every two minutes. But hierarchies were necessary evils: someone needed to be 'in charge' and accountable for anything going wrong. Note that in both of these early industrial revolutions, the focus remained within the organisation. The customer was simply an outsider who would buy a product and for whom the hierarchical operational model meant little – although it did make

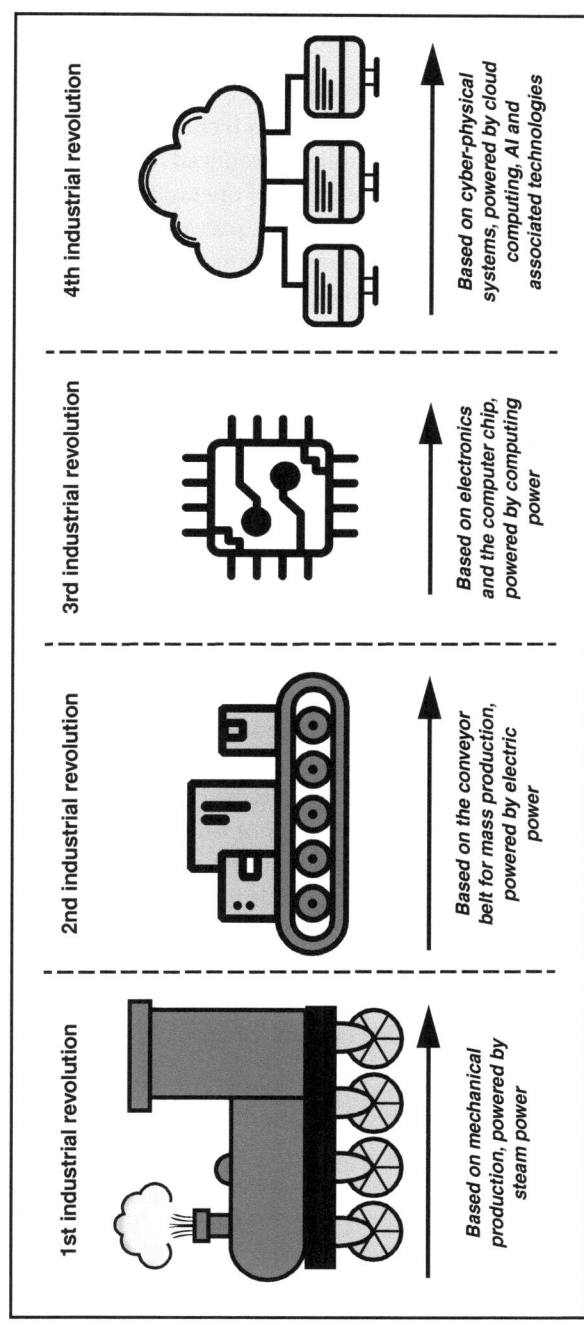

Figure 1.1 The evolution of the industrial operational models.

clear who a customer should complain to should they be unhappy about someone or something.

In the third industrial revolution, characterised by automation of tasks, electronics and information technology (IT), with the first programmable logic controller introduced in 1969, one would have thought that a shift in hierarchical operational models was imminent. It wasn't. In fact, it became prevalent. Somehow the computer also brought about newer forms of expressing hierarchy. For example, only some people could have a computer on their desks or access certain computer systems in the workplace. Organisations continued to be strongly hierarchical in their management approaches and the computer systems only reinforced the old operational models. Joseph Schumpeter reminds us that 'the new does not come out of the old, but appears next to the old, competes with him to the point of ruining him'. Only in this instance, it didn't ruin him but became glued to him. In fact, in some cases in the third industrial revolution, the computing systems became instruments of control, not simply new tools for work. A groundbreaking study by Shoshana Zuboff, published in 1988, illustrates this well. She had gained access to pulp mills that had installed new information systems for automating their work. As it turned out, those same machines simultaneously generated data that was useful for managers to know how individuals were working. Zuboff coined the term 'informate' – a twist on 'automate' – to illustrate how the technology was there not only to automate but also to inform. Surely, only managers at the top of the hierarchy would have access to such 'secondary' information from the machines. Hierarchies were here to stay. It afforded privilege to those at the top of organisational charts and created a drive in everyone else to try to reach the top, but for others there may have been a dark side (something we examine later in this book).

The challenges posed by these operational models with strong hierarchies during the third industrial revolution were unique, in that they exposed rigid structures and the unwillingness to change. The challenges were mainly those that created Napoleons and commoners within organisations. Positional power was wielded by those who were ranked high in the hierarchy. The entire model resulted in a system of distrust and favouritism, resulting in low motivation and a reluctance among those at the bottom of the ladder to take the initiative. The computer systems in many organisations did not necessarily help, in that they became instruments of control and surveillance within the organisation. Even if they weren't, such perceptions were often present. To address these challenges, researchers made calls to re-examine hierarchies and markers of hierarchies such as special offices for managers, parking spots, titles, desk sizes, and so on. These calls resulted in new open-plan office designs where everyone worked in the same flat office space, an idea that was meant to encourage interaction among colleagues irrespective of rank and to improve collaboration. However, it wasn't long after that each worker had their own cubicles within the open shared office space. It was also not uncommon to enter a large office space with several work colleagues but with a separate desk in the corner behind which would be (frequently) a male figurehead who was the boss. Hierarchical models persisted in these empires, filtering even into the fourth industrial revolution. In their frustration with these management models, Ted Coine and Mark Babbitt, in their 2014 book entitled *A World Gone Social: How Companies Must Adapt To Survive*, warned that organisations that continued to hold onto old hierarchical ideals faced extinction in this age of high technological advancement characterised by social media. The alarm bells that sounded were akin to Winston Churchill's words, 'Better to take the change by the hand before it takes us by the throat'.

The fourth industrial revolution of the twenty-first century is based on cyber-physical systems. At the core of its business models are the Internet of Things (IoT), Web 3.0, robotics, artificial intelligence (AI), augmented reality (AR) and its associated technologies, such as mixed/extended reality (XR) and virtual reality (VR), blockchain and cloud computing. The connectedness between humans and things that the fourth industrial revolution delivers, as well as the capabilities it bestows on all connected individuals (and things!), means that no one entity could be said to be privileged. The very architecture of the technologies underpinning the fourth industrial revolution is flat, so that all those who are connected by these technologies are welcome into a system where everyone or everything is on the same 'level'. For example, your fridge can now be connected to you, learning your habits and even placing orders by itself to refill on your behalf when it detects any shortage of items within it.

Your home can make its own decisions to cook you a meal using a recipe that you may not even have heard of. Of course, it is not as though you have lost control, as you can programme what you want from your connected devices, but the idea is that even the non-human things can think *alongside* you and, in some cases, *for* you. Where, then, is the hierarchy? In those scenarios where non-human things are making decisions for you, are you still in control and on top of the hierarchy? Have Winston Churchill's words not come true, that change will take you by the throat if you don't take it by the hand? It is at this junction that organisations find themselves in the twenty-first century as their empires fall.

In other words, the fourth industrial revolution poses an essential question to those who inhabit it: to change as their operating environment changes or to become obsolete by refusing to change? While somewhat stark, this need to evolve is not new. It occurred in previous eras as the cyclical nature of the ebb and flow of economic periods. Consider the Industrial Age, a 'round hole' economy utilising 'square peg' workers who, no matter their original unique shape and talent, were neither warranted nor rewarded for individuality, but for assimilation and collective productivity – meaning that, over time, the squarest of 'square peg' workers lost their edges to 'fit in' by being moulded into a 'round hole' responsibility. Henry Ford, a sizeable employer of the time, would often complain, 'Why is it when I hire a pair of hands, I get a human being as well?' Clearly the focus was on the productivity of the hired hands, without much thought to the entirety of the person. Such sentiment led Max Weber to note that workers of the era were entirely replaceable, just like the machines they operated. Karl Marx recognised this relationship within the *Economic and Philosophic Manuscripts of 1844* (1965) as alienated labour, proposing that work is supposed to increase a human's value, but in reality, it does the opposite. According to Marx, the devaluation of the human world grows in direct proportion to the increase in value of the world of things. To be clear, we are not Marxists, but the point raised is arguably a good assessment when we consider how hierarchies become potentially flattened by the fourth industrial revolution.

Conversely, this period is characterised by the fusion of technologies and people. Continuing to organise work solely for mass production without factoring in the economic as well as socio-technological changes of the day puts your organisation at risk of obsolescence. Stand-alone products and industries have been replaced by more integrated ecosystems, leading to a mesh of technologies and blurring the lines between the physical, digital and biological spheres owned by the biggest, most potent, fastest-growing and disruptive organisations in the world. These billion-dollar corporations have capitalised on the rapid penetration of the mobile Internet, facilitating the economic transition from the product economy to a platform economy. For instance, brands synonymous with products, such as Nike, have added digital platforms and membership components to engage customers beyond the physical retail, as the competitive landscape expands from traditional brick-and-mortar companies to digital marketplaces that threaten to pull consumer attention away from them.

Here are some examples of companies that have evolved with the changing times and the opportunities offered within the bigger ecosystem. As of 2022, Apple has the largest market capitalisation globally and is responsible for the total disruption of the music industry and the creation of home computing as we know it – but it's an easy mistake to think of Apple as a product brand. They do sell a lot of gadgets, but the iPod didn't change the music industry: iTunes – a platform – did. Likewise, the iPhone's beauty and processor speed weren't the driving force behind its success: the App Store – a platform – was. Consider Uber, too, which has become the world's largest taxi firm without owning a single car. And what about Facebook? Despite its critics, it is a hugely successful human-made creation, with followers increasing daily. These all speak to a move towards ecosystem thinking, where a multiplicity of actors are at play in order to make the business model successful. In other words, it is not simply about selling a product. It is about engaging with the array of various players that could make that product or service become dominant or sustained in the market space. This thinking moves away from who's on top or at the bottom towards how you can leverage the positioning and capability of others in your network to make your business model work. Ecosystems don't give hierarchies priority, whether that be in individual organisations or within the broader network of players involved; ecosystems create and thrive on interconnections.

According to Walid Negm, Chief Research and Innovation Officer, Capgemini Engineering:

> If you look at any emerging or major technology transition, whether that is electric vehicles, vertical flight, 5G, or fintech, it is very evident that both mind share and market share favour companies that take a co-existence approach like Apple, Uber and Facebook – building and shaping industry standards and being a synergetic part of the restructuring of value chains. However, to pursue new ideas, new ways of thinking, or new business models, there is a need for even more intensity – in a fast and frugal way. The objectives for a company are to link back to a diversity of players that cut across industry sectors, anchor onto technology platforms, and make sure value flows through the ecosystem's economy.

Negm's submission highlights keywords such as 'synergy', 'platforms' and 'diversity of players', which all allude to something beyond a singular organisation, i.e. a diverse collection of different players with which to work.

The fundamental realisation for leaders operating within the fourth industrial revolution is this: your ecosystem determines everything, and your customers are an integral part of that ecosystem, defining your competitive set and your relevance today. How is that? Your competitors are a click, scroll or keyword away. Without a compelling uniqueness and demonstrated relevance, your company risks being essentially equivalent, or worse, misunderstood. Hollywood learned that lesson the hard way, courtesy of Netflix and streaming. Your customer decides what matters most – and whether your organisation matters at all. If your organisation isn't unique and special – truly differentiated – in a way that matters to your customer, then guess what? You aren't even on their radar. They've scrolled past your offerings and moved on to more compelling options. It isn't about your business, its products or why you believe you matter. Your customers are asking themselves, 'Why should you matter to me?' Your customer should be the protagonist in your organisation's story (we discuss this in more detail in Chapters 3 and 4).

What is the implication of this in terms of how organisations are structured? While platforms like Facebook and others are thriving, top-down empires are dying. They can't survive in an environment where customers are increasingly fickle, supply chains are broken, competition is fierce and employees are stagnant. In a world that's moving faster and faster, with disruption around every corner, playing it safe is a risky strategy: $41 trillion in enterprise value is already exposed to disruption. So, to win big, organisations of all types must make a shift towards more flexible, networked structures to remain competitive. The empire is dead; long live the ecosystem.

Reimagining businesses as ecosystems

The rise of platforms is a natural offshoot of the freedom and speed of information enabled by new technologies and employees reclaiming power. It has shifted the balance of customer engagement from *caveat emptor* to *caveat venditor* – that is, *from 'let the buyer beware' to 'let the seller beware'*. The era of clearly bounded companies and industries is being overwritten by the trends towards re-platforming to the cloud and diverse Costa Rica-like ecosystems (first coined by Botanist Arthur Tansley in the 1930s) that have a revenue potential of over $66 trillion dollars in the next five years, because the customer is in charge. Customers increasingly demand personalisation rather than standardisation, as the old models of operations gradually lose relevance. This means that customers drive the multi-sided platforms, with users being interchangeably consumers and creators, buyers and sellers, readers and writers, etc. A term coined by Alvin Toffler that aptly describes this is *prosumers*. In other words, customers are not simply *consumers*, they are also *producers*. Indeed, the *prosumer* is here to stay. This gives rise to the concept of a business as an ecosystem, in which customers, employees and the organisation are deeply connected and highly dependent on one another (Figure 1.2).

In terms of trends, product brands and platform brands are one-sided or two-sided (multi-sided) markets, but ecosystem brands are co-evolutionary ecosystems seeking to turn *consumers* into *prosumers*. Ecosystem brands are distinct from the first two brand types, because whereas product brands emerged in the industrial economy and platform brands thrived on user traffic, ecosystem brands focus on creating user experience. As Haier Model Institute succinctly puts it: from the value perspective, product brands offer

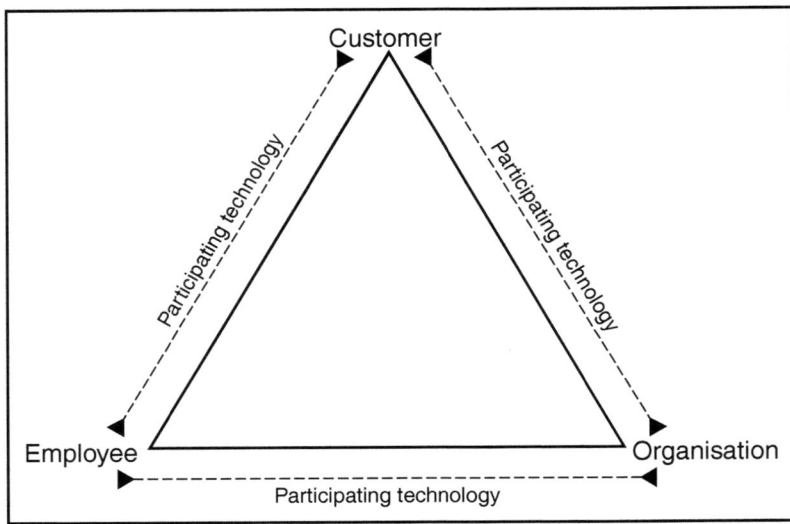

Figure 1.2 The interconnectedness of customers, employees and the organisation in a business ecosystem.

premium quality, platform brands offer premium traffic, but ecosystem brands provide ecosystem value. Thus, from a hardware era where 'the product is king' to an ecosystem era where the users are uniquely positioned, ecosystem brands attempt to create lifelong users. This is an essential ingredient for businesses to thrive in the fourth industrial revolution.

Platforms have consequently created ecosystems where customers can interact and are more engaged than ever before. As shown in Figure 1.2, the customer is now intricately woven into the fabric of the business ecosystem by virtue of what we call participating technologies. You can think of it as a houseguest who has now been given keys to the house so that they can come in at any time and choose to stay. While most people do not want guests to become forever tenants who refuse eviction, in this instance you need them to stay so you can continue to have your house in an attractive position. Those keys that your 'guests' now have in their possession are the participating technologies that enable them to unlock the doors to your house, to stay, leave or even destroy the house should they find you repulsive. Making your guests feel welcome brings an enjoyable level of engagement that keeps the house buzzing. Well, your 'guest' is your customer, only that, with ecosystem thinking, they are not guests but housemates who have keys. They come with a whole new level of engagement. This engagement brings new productivity, creating a developed efficiency and pace that fuel further commitment. As this gains traction, it can lead to exponential growth beyond the capabilities of traditional business models because it is now the 'ecosystem era'. The race is on to get as close to customers as possible and to do more for them than ever before. This motivation is consequently driving a radical rethink of how organisations interact with their customers and how their internal management structures enable more customer proximity. Thus, the 'ecosystem era' turns enterprises into innovative ecosystems that create valuable user experiences, where every person and object become a node in the ecosystem. (We examine the customer in greater detail in Chapter 3.) Now consider the following case studies that illustrate the reimagining of the business as an ecosystem with three interacting stakeholders at its core – the organisation, customers (users) and employees.

In SAP's case (Case Study 1.1), note how the thinking has moved away from a product-based to a network-enabled business model. Whereas the former focuses on product features that meet

Case Study 1.1

SAP prioritises a customer-centric business model

SAP, the enterprise tech company responsible for powering 8 out of 10 Fortune 500 companies, recognised the opportunity to help customers in a leap from product-based to network-enabled business models. They crafted a company vision aimed at transitioning traditional businesses into intelligent enterprises and connecting them to create the world's largest business network. 'COVID-19 was the nail in the coffin for static business processes as we knew them. There has never been a clearer need for real-time flexibility in how companies exchange goods, services, talent, assets, and data,' says Scott Russell, SAP Board member and Head of Customer Success.

customers' needs, the latter prioritises helping customers within the ecosystem to ensure that the solution meets their needs. This understanding takes into account the multiplicity of other factors that are connected to the customer's need within the ecosystem. This shift in focus cascaded through the entire organisation, including the company vision, enabling SAP to move away from static processes and incorporate flexibility into the exchange relationship with its customers.

In reimagining business as an ecosystem, Case Study 1.2 highlights the importance of participating technologies, in this instance, AI. The interesting thing here, as you would have noticed, is how the companies deployed AI. It was not aimed at product development or product competitiveness but at the employee experience. As illustrated in Figure 1.2, a business ecosystem thinking requires a focus on three important stakeholders, one of which is the employee. This way of thinking is as much employee-centric as it is customer-centric.

Case Study 1.2

Artificial intelligence for human resource management

Management scholar Ashish Malik and his team of researchers conducted a recent study on large technology firms that have implemented a complex ecosystem of platforms using artificial intelligence (AI) applications in the human resource management (HRM) function. It found that the HRM function was positively enhanced by AI-enabled applications offering a high-quality employee experience. Leveraging AI and related technologies, firms are employing hyper-personalised HR offerings based on employee attributes and needs. This has led to massive reductions in HR transactional volumes and created business efficiencies, while also improving employee experience in terms of job satisfaction, commitment and intention to quit. The authors note that through bundles of AI applications, businesses can elevate the overall employment experience of their employees.

However, it is not as though your own organisation must deploy AI. In fact, there may be some hesitation to plunge into AI-enabled human resource management (HRM), mainly because traditional corporate strategies, theories and analytical frameworks have become so entrenched that business leaders may opt to go with what is familiar. Nonetheless, in a business environment that is often characterised by volatility, uncertainty, complexity and ambiguity (VUCA), traditional academic theories and old practices are no longer able to provide accurate guidance. For example, Michael Porter's well-known competitive strategy deals with competition among enterprises and seeks the maximisation of long-term profits and return on investment for shareholders. The prevailing resource-based perspective underpinning his theory is based on the assumption that individual firms own assets that essentially determine their productive opportunities and competitive strategies. This perspective promotes command and control, which is typically found in pyramidal organisational structures, line management, layers of authority and traditional, rigid pathways of progression and reward.

From Porter's perspective, strategists would typically classify competitors as direct, indirect and substitute based on industry and market. But that rubric worked when everyone stayed in their lanes. However, the reality in a dynamic, platform-based era is that unique ownership is gradually becoming a thing of the past, as companies share platforms and ecosystems develop. Those formerly individualised lanes vanish with platform models because all members of the ecosystem share a customer-centric mindset. Tools like the SWOT analysis and Porter's industry analysis framework were created in a previous era with a set of assumptions and prevailing conditions. These tools have merit; however, they need to be applied to a different context, taking into consideration the dynamic nature of the ecosystem era and the gradual shift in business mindset from direct competition to collaboration.

In the current era, companies routinely leap over industry boundaries in search of market share and profit margin, breaking free from outdated assumptions, such as the thinking that industry boundaries define competitive strategy. Your customer doesn't care about your industry. They care about what matters to them. Consider how content wars illustrate these new realities. Hollywood never expected to compete with TikTok, much less Amazon and Netflix. The films and their stars owned the screen for decades, and despite this, today's consumer has stronger buyer power – being able to switch easily from one content provider to another. Consequently, companies have shifted from describing 'what we do' to illustrating 'why we matter'. Today's consumers are the heroes of their own story, curating life on their terms courtesy of social media and search engine optimisation. They seek an emotional connection and expect to be valued as whole persons in their natural habitats. Your company's differentiation success depends on the ability to answer this question: 'Why should your company, product or service matter to me?' Capturing someone's attention, even for a moment, is the new currency in the age of social commerce. This is certainly the case, as Nicholas Carr discusses in his 2008 article 'Is Google making us stupid?', highlighting our ephemeral attention spans as he considers what the Internet has done to our brains. Capturing the attention of your employees as well as your customers is thus crucial in this new era.

While some businesses and sectors have moved on to operate in the ecosystem era, others are still far behind, mainly due to a lack of understanding of how their organisation can evolve such that it utilises the opportunities available in an interconnected ecosystem. For those organisations that have leveraged the available opportunities in the business ecosystem, the verdict is out as we see huge leaps in performance; in fact, new business models have emerged with IoT, AI and other participating technologies within the ecosystem. However, there are several other organisations that need to consider alternative approaches to doing business. The value of an ecosystem approach to society can be illustrated in the symbiotic relationship among all the players involved. For instance, business ecosystems have seen increased collaboration between educational and research institutions, industry and government. According to Matthew Tirrell, Dean of the Pritzker School of Molecular Engineering at the University of Chicago:

> Universities can only take their discoveries and inventions to a certain point beyond which much more massive effort and scale-up are required to bring useful solutions to society. There's a need to accelerate research to advance technological innovations that can be quickly commercialised on a global scale. This

requires a robust infrastructure and mutual understanding of goals and objectives that connect academia to industry and research to the public. When universities, industry and government work together, we can develop solutions that address some of society's biggest challenges much faster than when we go it alone. Without this ecosystem, the potential of emerging technologies could be limited.

As we argued earlier, old habits die hard and many business leaders are still stuck in the old ways, particularly in relation to running hierarchical and uniquely bounded organisations. Our research at Haier has shown it is possible to make that needed shift and evolve in response to changing operational environments. It takes courage, and you as a leader must be willing to take that first step. For example, Zhang Ruimin, who led Haier's transition, was courageous enough to face established organisational structures and systems and remoulded these into what was fit for purpose. In other words, having a new understanding of the value of an interconnected ecosystem led to the dismantling of structures that inhibit rather than encourage the flexibility needed for successful collaboration between employees, customers (users) and the organisation. To make this possible at Haier – the world's largest white goods manufacturer – in 2005 CEO Zhang Ruimin adopted the philosophy of RenDanHeYi, at the core of which is the idea of 'zero distance to the customer' (we explore this philosophy further in Chapter 2). Distance, in this case, is not literal but refers to the regularity of interactions with the customer and the amplification of influence via social networks that connect Haier to its customers as shown in the business ecosystem (see Figure 1.2).

Chapter summary, reflective questions and practical implications

In this first chapter, we hope you have been challenged to think about where your own organisation is heading. Are you still running as an empire, or making the transition to a new way of working in your business ecosystem? Be aware that this requires significant time in reassessing your organisation and its place within the business ecosystem. More importantly, any change you wish to make requires reflecting on your own practice as a manager. Here are a few reflective questions for you to consider:

- *How do you really see your organisation's structure?* Your hierarchical model may need serious rethink. Empower your team, not just a few individuals 'at the top', by rewarding risk-taking by those who were once at the bottom of your hierarchy and slowly changing the mindset of your organisation as you flatten the hierarchy.
- *Are you abreast of technological developments that can potentially impact your business?* Your participating technologies may need to be updated to sustain your organisation in the fourth industrial revolution. Identify ongoing technological advancements (employee-related or economic) which may affect (or have affected) the continuity of your current business model. Beware of falling into the trap of keeping up with the Joneses. Not every technological development is for you.
- *Who are the members of your ecosystem that you can partner with?* Think about potential partnerships which can offer synergies that would form the foundation of your ecosystem. Remember, in a business ecosystem, it is not necessarily about you being on top, but about your network of relationships that help you accomplish your respective goals.
- *Are you aware of your organisation's core strengths and competencies?* Be clear about your strengths and what you as an organisation bring to the table. Knowing this will help you to align with those players that complement you within the ecosystem.
- *What philosophy drives how you run your business?* Before you move on to the next chapter, think about your current business philosophy and how it is challenged by the fourth industrial revolution.

Bibliography

Bennett, N. & Lemoine, G. J. (2014) 'What VUCA really means for you', *Harvard Business Review*, available at https://hbr.org/2014/01/what-vuca-really-means-for-you (accessed 19 August 2022).

Carr, N. (2008) 'Is Google making us stupid? What the Internet is doing to our brains', available at https://www.theatlantic.com/

magazine/archive/2008/07/is-google-making-us-stupid/ 306868/ (accessed 18 August 2022).

Coine, T. & Babbitt, M. (2014) *A world gone social: how companies must adapt to survive.* New York, NY: AMACOM.

Deloitte report (2018) *The rise of the platform economy,* available at https://www2.deloitte.com/content/dam/Deloitte/nl/Documents/ humancapital/deloitte-nl-hc-the-rise-of-the-platform-economy-report.pdf (accessed 19 August 2022).

Greenberg, S. (2012) *Building organizations that work,* available at https://www.gsb.stanford.edu/insights/building-organizations-work (accessed 18 August 2022).

Haier Model Research Institute (2022), available at http://www.haierresearch.com/home

Harteis, C. (2018) *The impact of digitalization in the workplace. An educational view.* Springer International Publishing.

Malik, A., Budhwar, P., Patel, C. & Srikanth, N. R. (2022) 'May the bots be with you! Delivering HR cost-effectiveness and individualised employee experiences in an MNE', *The International Journal of Human Resource Management,* 33(6): 1148–1178.

Marx, K., Milligan, M., Struik, D. J., Bottomore, T. B. & Fromm, E. (1965) 'The Economic and Philosophic Manuscripts of 1844', *Science and Society,* 29(3): 357–362.

Moazed, A. & Johnson, N. L. (2016) *Modern monopolies: what it takes to dominate the 21st century economy.* St Martin's Press.

Porter, M. E. (1990) *The competitive advantage of nations.* The Free Press.

Schumpeter, J. (1934). *The theory of economic development: an inquiry into profits, capital, credit, interest, and the business cycle* (translated from the German by Redvers Opie). Cambridge MA: Harvard University Press.

Shendruk, A. & McDonnell, T. (n.d.) *How much is an ecosystem worth?,* available at https://qz.com/1792563/how-much-is-an-ecosystem-worth/ (accessed 14 November 2022).

Tansley, A. G. (1935) 'The use and abuse of vegetational concepts and terms', *Ecology.* 16(3): 284–307. doi:10.2307/1930070

Toffler, A. (1980) *The third wave.* New York: William Morrow.

Sledgehammers, optional

Introduction

In this chapter, we examine the management philosophy with which you can navigate the business ecosystem. We take a deep dive into the Chinese philosophy of RenDanHeYi (RDHY) as it intricately interconnects the three key players we have highlighted earlier (see Chapter 1), i.e. employees, customers (users) and the organisation, which together form what we refer to as the RenDanHeYi triad. We discuss how they fit into ecosystems of sustainable value as well as the opportunities and benefits of adopting the model. We illustrate the concepts with examples and case study organisations on how this unique philosophy has changed the face of management like a sledgehammer that flattens hierarchical models of management practice.

The story of RenDanHeYi

A new manager once received customer complaints about the quality of his refrigerator factory's goods. He asked the employees to destroy every faulty refrigerator with a sledgehammer. The manager told the team that, from then on, they would be known as a company that met customers' expectations. Over the next 30 years, that manager, Zhang Ruimin, would become the chairperson of that same company, Haier Group (Haier), valued at $18.7 billion and recognised worldwide as the largest home appliance company in the world. Since its inception in 1984, the company under the leadership of Zhang Ruimin has been on such a journey. What began as a modest refrigerator business with only seven workers and one product has now grown into a worldwide behemoth with over 70,000 employees and millions of products. Haier's secret to success? A relentless focus on innovation and a deep understanding of what their customers want and need.

27

Haier's journey began in the mid-1980s when China was still a largely closed economy. The country was in the midst of a massive economic transformation, and Haier was able to capitalise on this by producing quality products that were affordable for the average Chinese consumer. In the early 1990s, Haier began to expand beyond China's borders, first into Southeast Asia and then into Europe and North America. When the first modern refrigerator was introduced to the market, it became an instant hit. The company that manufactured this revolutionary appliance saw their sales go through the roof. Although Haier's success is due in part to its aggressive expansion strategy, the company has also been able to achieve impressive growth because of its focus on innovation. Haier has long been an advocate of 'open innovation', which is a philosophy that emphasises the importance of collaboration and sharing of ideas. This philosophy has allowed Haier to tap into the collective wisdom of its employees, customers and partners to create better products and solutions.

Haier's success is not simply due to its cutting-edge technologies or efficient production process. It owes a lot of its success to its unique organisational structure and culture when it comes to the 'ecosystem organisation'. This is founded on three key concepts: (i) value generation for everyone; (ii) constant change; and (iii) win–win collaboration. Haier's organisational structure and culture are based on these ideals, which are truly implemented, not simply words or sentiments. Everyone has the *freedom* to take action and generate value they espouse. In effect, this allows people in the company to try new things without fear. Little permission is sought from someone higher up and, as a result, they experiment freely and are encouraged to do so.

The traditional hierarchical organisation may be great at getting things done but it is weak in terms of facilitating creativity and innovation. The ecosystem organisation flips this conventional paradigm upside down by putting more emphasis on value creation for everyone. In an ecosystem organisation, everyone is a leader and everyone is responsible for generating value. This sort of structure allows for more creativity and innovation because people are not restricted by hierarchy. The ecosystem organisation is also based on the principle of constant change. In a traditional organisation, change could often be seen as something to be cautious about or perhaps avoided. But in an ecosystem organisation, change is embraced as a necessary part of doing business. This is because it acknowledges that the world is constantly changing and you need to keep pace with it. Haier knows this and believes it needs to change with the changing environment in order to stay ahead of the curve. In other words, the ecosystem organisation is constantly evolving and, for this, Haier looks for ways to improve and evolve. This philosophy is somewhat evident in the company's products, as new technological developments are always incorporated into newer products. It is also evident in the way that Haier organises its work. For example, the company has implemented a 'flat' organisational structure, which means that there are no hierarchical layers or titles. This flat structure allows for more direct communication and collaboration among its employees.

Our research into Haier reveals communities of employees who autonomously connect with other actors to form their own ecosystems. Haier calls these *ecosystem micro-communities* (EMCs). These are set up by employees who wish to express their individuality and drive an aspect of the business. The EMC is focused on a particular product line and grows as new customer needs are uncovered. For instance, an EMC can be formed to take charge of the organisation's Internet of Food (IoF) business or its Smart Kitchen business and so on. This establishes a culture for both new and existing employees who wish to take control of their own future or run their own mini-company under the bigger umbrella of Haier. A range of people constitute members of the EMC ecosystem and include users, suppliers, farmers, partner organisations and other EMCs with complementary product lines. In this way, while the EMC could be seen as a stand-alone unit, in reality it is connected in a web-like structure to a wider ecosystem where information is constantly being shared in order to continue to develop solutions to user needs, sometimes necessitating the creation of an offspring EMC (see Figure 2.1).

To illustrate, take for instance Haier's Smart Kitchen EMC. It is connected to various other entities like furniture companies, digital technology companies, chefs, the IoF EMC and so on. In other words, this Smart Kitchen EMC is effective in how it organises all the resources it needs within the ecosystem to fulfil its business needs. A customer might want a kitchen fitted but not with all the

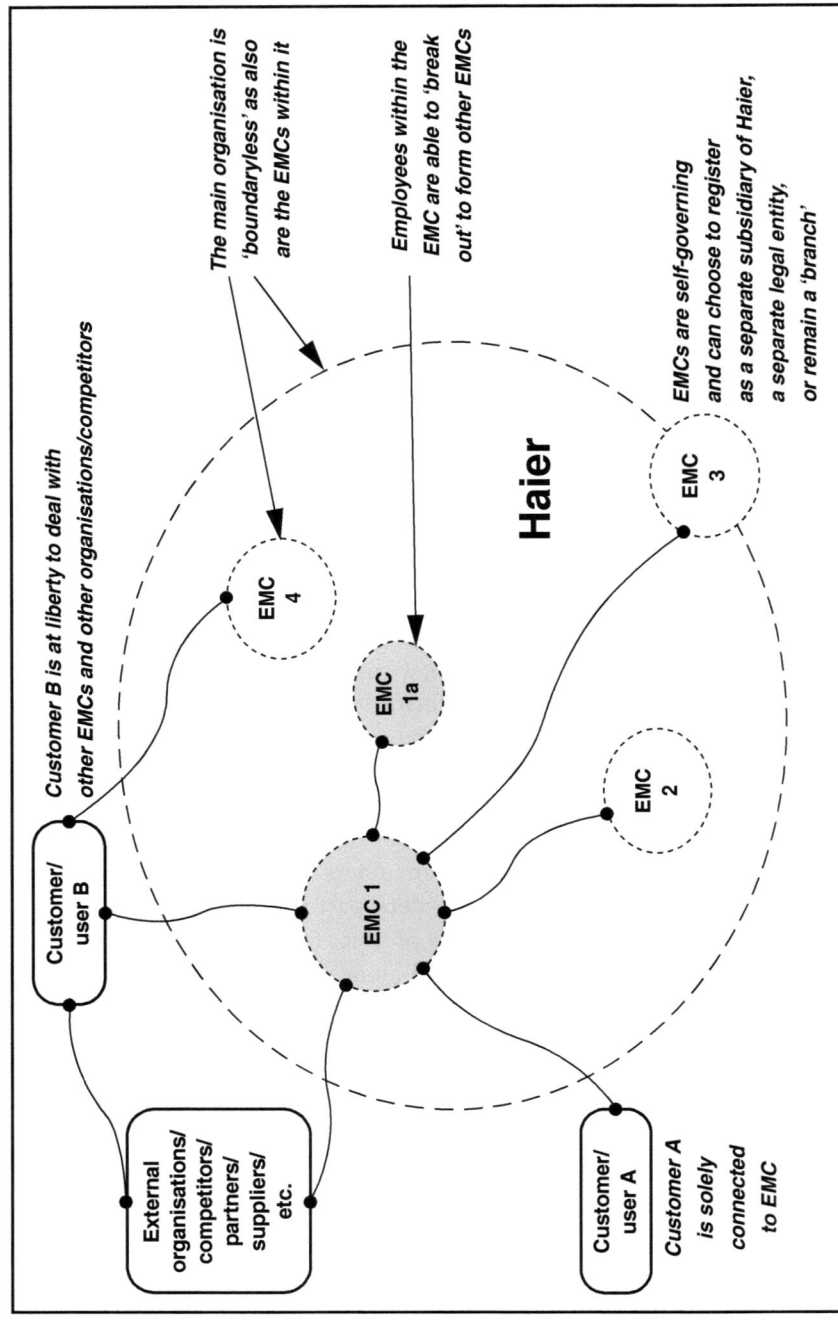

Figure 2.1 Haier's ecosystem micro-communities (EMCs).

technologies that make it 'smart', and this EMC would still be able to deliver this product and maintain the customer relationship just in case the smart components are needed in the future.

The EMC in this case ensures that its objectives take into account all the connections it needs for its operations. Without such ecosystem thinking, an EMC would not be possible. In operating this Smart Kitchen EMC, employees may need to collaborate with the Washing Machine EMC or the Fridge EMC etc. in order to provide a 'complete' service to the customer. Several of these EMCs are run by entrepreneurial individuals within Haier who are empowered to make decisions for themselves, plan their own activities, innovate in ways that were not before thought possible, and so on. Who would have thought that Haier, an electronics giant, also now deals in furniture? Well, its Smart Kitchen EMC has tentacles that reach that domain. The potential for growth is thus limitless as new user needs drive the emergence of new EMCs and product lines.

The Haier Corporation's management and culture are two of the reasons for its success. Haier's dedication to creating value for everyone, continuous change and win–win cooperation has allowed it to carve out its own unique managerial climate. These principles have also permitted Haier to leverage its employees, clients and partners' collective knowledge to create even more value. Haier understands that it cannot do everything alone and that it needs to partner with other organisations in order to be successful. It has therefore built a vast network of partners and suppliers with whom it works closely to create the best products possible. This win–win philosophy extends beyond just business partnerships, to its employees, as it believes in the need to create value for everyone. We find that at the core of all these ideals is the company's management philosophy, RenDanHeYi.

The RenDanHeYi model

In the word RenDanHeYi, *Ren* refers to employees, but these are not limited to people within a particular unit of the business; rather, the term includes anyone who comes up with a competitive proposal to join or lead a project. In RDHY, employees are not seen as passive executors of orders, but as being actively involved in

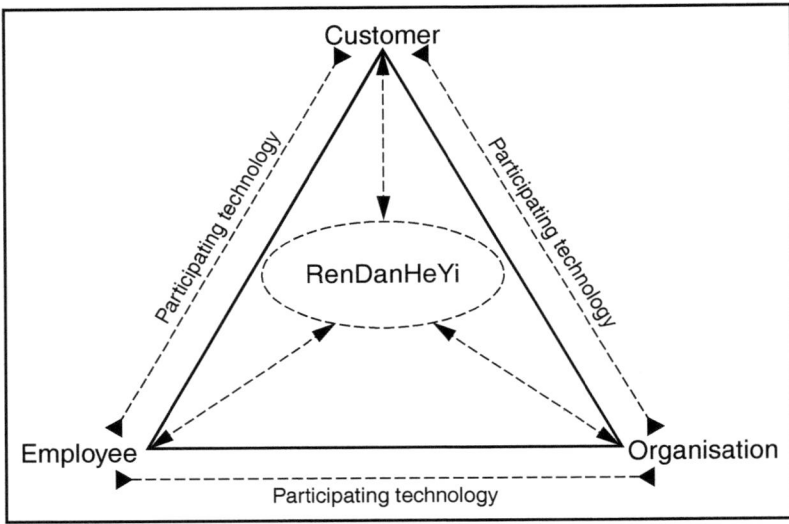

Figure 2.2 The RenDanHeYi triad: three key players, intrinsically networked and interconnected.

entrepreneurship through a dynamic partnership with the three key members of the triad (shown in Figure 2.2). Employees are involved in the management of the organisation and in decisions about business, people and compensation. *Dan* refers to user value and it describes a bid for, rather than an assignment from the top of the organisational hierarchy, which also reinforces the active role of the employee in the organisation. *HeYi* captures the alignment between the value created for users and the profit, which can then be shared by all involved. In other words, employees under RDHY are expected to focus on creating user value, which translates into profit they all share in.

In most hierarchical organisations, employee compensation is often tied to position and seniority. The job of employees is to execute orders and thereafter receive performance evaluations from their superiors, while the enterprise as a whole receives the profits from which it pays compensation to employees. In RDHY, the reward system is quite different. Employees are accountable for creating user value and their performance is rewarded accordingly. This is often measured by evaluations received from customers, who we also refer to as users. The share of the profit that employees receive is therefore directly related to evaluation of the value created. This dynamic alters the relationship between an organisation and its employees, given the symbiotic engagement between the employee and the customer.

The task for the organisation is to enable a functional network involving itself, its customers, and its employees. The organisation is to be a catalyst for positive engagements by providing a 'platform' for continuous engagement across all three players. In this way, purely transactional interactions are transformed into interconnected relationships characterised by ongoing, personalised and responsive interactions. Such interaction allows for immediate feedback, critiquing of ideas and a stronger sense of purpose and satisfaction to employees. This gives a sense of autonomy and a feeling that a business is being run within a business. These self-driven and interconnected groups of autonomous enterprises explain why Haier was able to achieve growth during the COVID-19 pandemic, despite a downturn in the home appliances industry in major global markets: in the first quarter of 2021, Haier's global turnover and profit increased by 28.7% and 104% year-on-year, respectively. Using this revolutionary model, Haier has created an interconnected ecosystem of customer–employee–organisation interactions, including 71 research institutes, 30 industrial parks, 122 manufacturing centres and over 230,000 sales networks worldwide, and has created more than 1.6 million new jobs.

Beliefs underpinning the RenDanHeYi philosophy

The human-centric goal of RDHY turns 'economic persons' into 'autonomous persons.' Thus, RDHY strives to create a 'rainforest' rather than a 'walled garden' as Haier's Zhang Ruimin puts it. This is accomplished by connecting the dots between users, businesses and things to create an ecology of co-creation and value sharing – hence the 'walled garden' metaphor for describing the modern business ecosystem. In a 'rainforest', there is no need to sacrifice human initiative and creativity in the name of efficiency. Instead, people are autonomous beings who are allowed self-expression. Unfortunately, businesses today are often like 'walled gardens', with rules and regulations aimed at making that walled garden self-sustaining. This is not necessarily a bad thing as, after all, various businesses have been successful with such underpinning systems. The challenge, however, is that a walled garden closes off cross-fertilisation from outside its walls. In other words, the vast potential for creative interconnections that would encourage creativity is limited. In an era of the Internet of Things, openness is key to surviving within a business ecosystem. In fact, in some cases it is demanded by customers who want transparency at every level of business operations. In RDHY, the worldview is to see the business environment as an ecosystem, a rainforest in which individuality-in-concert-with-others as a belief system is operational.

Western ideas about management have been dominant in both academic and practitioner domains for several decades. The RDHY management principles, however, are somewhat different, requiring a change in paradigm. The philosophy is based on a series of beliefs associated with the idea that every individual has potential and can be developed. It empowers employees, believing that they can make decisions on their own. Such autonomy means that the underpinning practices are not about telling people what they should do, or how, but about allowing self-expression. This employee-centric approach is also coupled with customer-centricity in that RDHY believes in the voice of the customer. This may seem obvious, but it is actually quite radical (as we explain in Chapters 3 and 4). Most companies focus on shareholder value above all else, which can lead to decisions that put profits ahead of customers' needs. Haier flips this script, putting customers at the centre as they are considered key players in the ecosystem. That might mean making decisions that don't maximise profits in the short term, but ultimately result in a better experience for customers and more loyalty in the long run. Of course, this isn't to say that you should not focus on making money. But when it comes to making decisions, the customer's needs should be given serious consideration. This philosophy can be applied in a number of ways. For example, a company might focus on creating a great customer service experience, even if it means spending more money than its competitors. Or it might make sure its products are of the highest quality, even if that means charging more. Ultimately, taking into account the customer's needs is all about creating long-term relationships built on trust and mutual respect. And that's something any company can benefit from. Happy customers are the life blood of your company – it only makes sense to keep them close to you.

The second belief in RDHY is that every employee has the potential to be creative and contribute to the company's success. This idea is reflected in Haier's flat organisational structure, which allows workers more freedom to invent. As we have highlighted earlier, this type of structure eliminates hierarchical layers, giving employees more direct access to decision-makers and allowing for quicker communication and decision-making. There are many advantages to flat organisation structures. First, they promote open communication and collaboration among employees. Second, they give employees a greater sense of ownership and responsibility for their work. And third, they allow businesses to be more agile and responsive to change. Despite these advantages, flat organisation structures are not without their challenges. Without clear hierarchical lines, it can sometimes be difficult to know who is responsible for what tasks. As a result, there can be a lack of accountability. The key is to ensure that processes are put in place to counter these challenges while empowering everyone in the organisation.

The third belief in RDHY is that of continuous improvement. This means your organisation must have the willingness to do research and aim to try new ideas. In order to maintain a competitive edge, businesses must continually strive for creativity and innovation. By innovation we mean both product and process innovation. It is an understanding that it is not necessarily about new products but also about how things are done within your organisation. Encouraging creativity and innovation within your workforce can be a challenge, but it is essential for success – for example, encouraging open-mindedness and out-of-the-box thinking; fostering an environment of collaboration and knowledge sharing; encouraging risk-taking (sometimes the best ideas come from failures); rewarding creative thinking and innovative solutions; and being open to change (the only constant is change itself!). After all, by encouraging creativity and innovation, you will give your business the best chance for success.

The fourth belief in RDHY is that talent should be respected and given their due. This means valuing employees for their skills and abilities, not just their seniority or position within the company. Talent management autonomy can be a difficult concept to grasp, but it's important to understand in order to manage your team properly. Autonomy refers to the ability of individuals to make decisions and take actions without direct supervision. In other words, it's the freedom to work independently. There are several benefits of granting autonomy to your team members. First, it allows them to use their creativity and knowledge to solve problems and complete tasks. Second, it motivates them to do their best work, as they know that their decisions will have an impact on the final product or outcome. Finally, it builds trust between you and your team members, as they feel that you trust their abilities and judgement.

The fifth belief in RDHY is that an entrepreneurial spirit is essential for success. This means encouraging employees to think like entrepreneurs, even if they're not running their own businesses. This is the entrepreneurial mindset. Individuals who are willing to take risks and innovate are often the ones who reap the rewards. The entrepreneurial mindset is, we believe, something everyone can develop through experience and education. You are not necessarily born with it, in which case others would be said to lack it. You can build it. Period. In fact, all those 'nature versus nurture' arguments are outdated in the twenty-first century where everyone can be who they want to be. There are a few key traits that all successful entrepreneurs share, such as determination and resilience. If you're looking to boost your entrepreneurial skill set, there are a few things you can do. First, seek out opportunities to learn from more experienced entrepreneurs. This could involve reading books or articles on the topic, attending workshops or seminars, or even shadowing someone in a business leadership role. Additionally, try to surround yourself with like-minded individuals who can provide support and encouragement. Finally, don't be afraid to take risks – remember, failure is often the best teacher. This is rooted in RDHY management practice.

The sixth and final belief in RDHY is that change is always possible. This means that no matter how successful a company is, there's always room for improvement. Companies can always find ways to optimise their operations and improve their bottom line. For instance, you can focus on your customer service. This means being responsive to customer needs and providing a high level of service. Another area to think about is employee satisfaction. Happy employees are more productive and more likely to stick around. Create an environment where employees feel valued and appreciated. This can be done by providing better training for employees, implementing customer feedback systems, and offering more convenient and responsive customer service options (we discuss this topic in more detail in Chapter 5).

These six beliefs that underpin RDHY can form the foundation of your own management philosophy. They must become embedded in the organisation and implemented at various levels of your operations in order to realise the benefits.

The opportunities and benefits of adopting RenDanHeYi

The RDHY model as simplified in Figure 2.2 offers a toolkit that you can use in your own management practice. We are not proposing in this chapter that you follow everything to the letter without due consideration for your own context. In fact, we found, in our own research of this management practice, that its implementation is nuanced within Haier's several subsidiaries. What you'll find in Haier Japan is not exactly the same as what you will see expressed in Haier China or at General Electric Appliances (owned by Haier) in the United States. What this means is that there are opportunities for you to take on the principles to apply in your own context. As discussed earlier, there are four elements in RDHY's bloodline: the organisation, employees, customers and participating technology. These four elements provide specific opportunities for you to take advantage of. Whereas the first – your own organisation – is unique and therefore we are unable to show you the specifics of what's possible, the other three are generic commonalities with which you can craft something amazing for your company. In the area of employees, we go deeper in Chapter 5. For your customers, we delve into this in Chapters 3, 4 and 7 with the complexity it deserves. And throughout the book, we highlight participating technologies, specifics of which are seen in the following chapters. With that in mind, the opportunities and benefits of adopting RDHY range from the personal through to wider impacts on the ecosystem. At the personal level, we look at recent research led by management expert Vijay Pereira on multi-level innovative ecosystems. This large study was conducted in a Chinese multinational enterprise to ascertain the strategies deployed through disruptive global expansion and growth. With a focus at the individual level, the researchers found 14 managerial competencies that reflect what we also found in our in-depth study of Haier. What this means is that there are inherent benefits for managers deploying principles of RDHY in their practice, as they have opportunities for personal growth and professional development along the lines of these competencies. It also allows for organisational growth throughout the ecosystem. These competencies are as shown in Table 2.1.

Table 2.1 Fourteen competencies as opportunities for personal growth in RDHY.

Agility	You want to be able to quickly identify and adapt to the changing business environment as the ecosystem is a constantly evolving one.
Entrepreneurial intelligence	You should be able to start something new in an intrapreneurial way and be ready to experiment with new things.
Business acumen	A customer-centric and employee-centric approach does not preclude an attention to profit, without which you will be out of business.
Design thinking	A customer-centric approach means you should offer what your customers say they need, not what you think they want. Design thinking pays attention to the customer's own needs and listens to the user.
Disruptive leadership	Be ready to lead change in flattening your hierarchy and challenging others in your team to reward innovation, not seniority.
Collaborative mindset	This requires an openness to work with even those in the ecosystem you might consider as your competitors.
Problem-solving and decision-making	Your ecosystem has emergent needs and you must be ready to solve problems from multiple perspectives without looking for the 'perfect' solution; when you have an optimal solution, be bold in your decision-making.

Research orientation	Your active presence with your customers is crucial for building a strong research orientation. You don't wait for queries or suggestions; you go looking for them. This is what will feed into your R&D operations and makes your organisation a constantly growing one.
Connected technology architecture	If your participating technologies are not connecting your customers and your employees, you are doing it all wrong.
Data analytics	A human-centric philosophy of management does not mean you throw your numbers out of the window; in fact, all adopters of RDHY also have analytics at the core of their activities.
Project leadership	This is not simply the management of a project but is an opportunity to conceptualise and initiate new projects with your employees.
Robotic process automation	Remember that because your focus is on your employees and customers, you may want to automate the repetitive, dull and often time-consuming tasks so you can redeploy your human resources to what is more important.
Digital intelligence and modelling	The business ecosystem of the twenty-first century is one whose lifeline is digital technology. Either be digital-savvy and model your business accordingly or become a digital immigrant and learn about this new ecosystem you are now a part of. Digital immigrants are those who have had to learn new digital technologies altogether and most managers fall into this category.
Sustainability	There is the urgent need to consider how your own business is having an impact on the ecosystem and the wider world. By all means be sustainable in your business model, but think carefully about how you are contributing to the environment as a whole.

These set of 14 managerial competencies provide you with a toolkit to identify which areas need to be worked on, which your employees need to be trained in, and which your business needs to be developed in. The researchers argue that this set of competencies is a complex phenomenon that spans multiple technologies and requires an extensive set of capabilities that managers and organisations need to develop in their functional and business contexts. For organisations that practise RDHY, these competencies provide opportunities for personal growth at the managerial level as well as organisational growth at the ecosystem level. For instance, the management strategies suited for an ecosystem of smart factories would have to consider *connected technology architecture* (one of the 14 competencies) that involves customers as much as it does the supply chain feeding the smart factory. Adopting RDHY is a call to action and an opportunity for growth. It challenges you but its principles offer benefits, as we show in the various examples and case studies used in this book. Take, for instance, the example of Xiaomi in Pereira's research on innovative ecosystems (see Case Study 2.1).

Case Study 2.1

Xiaomi

The story of Xiaomi, the Chinese telecommunications firm, is told at the post-entry stage of its internationalisation strategy into India. As a new entrant, Xiaomi was confronted by risks in the new ecosystem, which they had to take steps to address. To do so, they pre-empted, managed and mitigated the risks found in foreign markets over various stages of the life cycles of the organisation's subsidiaries within its innovative ecosystem through a complex set of strategies that depended on managerial competencies mentioned above in various areas. These competencies were developed as a result of the experiences they gained in four distinct phases of their entry into this foreign market: pre-entry (when decisions on mode of entry are made), immediate post-entry, current status, and future strategies and plans. Research conducted within the company showed that by demonstrating *agility*, Xiaomi navigated the complex landscape of its host market by exploiting the ecosystem and adopting unique, contextually relevant strategies that would later aid in its management of risk in the Indian market.

Xiaomi in India managed to embed itself within the ecosystem of its host country through leveraging the various connections it established. We also find that in Haier – an RDHY-practising organisation – connections within its ecosystems matter. In fact, ecosystem connections matter so much that the organisation ensures its participating technologies are built specifically to ensure this. A good way to ensure you are functioning well within your ecosystem is to measure your connections as a baseline and continuously monitor changes or growth in your ecosystem connections. For instance, a simple experiment of who is connected to whom within your ecosystem mapped onto a flipchart will help you to identify the strength of your connections and the gaps that must be filled. If you see several connections to any particular individual or department as a whole, this may be indicative of where your key 'nodes' are within your organisation. You can then take steps to ensure a uniform spread of connections by challenging managers and employees to establish the needed connections that they didn't have before. See it as a way of creating uniformity in how your value chain is connected to you. Should one manager resign, would you still be able to continue with the connections he or she had? A baseline measure of your connections is always a starting point for a new kind of conversation within your ecosystem. A few years ago, one of us conducted this exercise with a group of managers in a Fortune 200 organisation. At the workshop, all managers were asked to write down the names of the people they believed were absolutely crucial to their work within their ecosystem and to show why. These were all then mapped onto flipcharts and arranged on a whiteboard. At the end of the workshop, it was clear some managers needed to connect with other entities/individuals/organisations within their bigger ecosystem in order to fill the gaps they had in their own work. The key to doing this exercise is to ask why those connections were absolutely crucial and to build strategies for sustaining them.

The building of connections within your ecosystem is a key benefit of an RDHY-practising organisation, especially as we have witnessed fallouts of business closure and loss of customer base that stem from the COVID-19 pandemic. It is now time to regain lost connections and rebuild customer bases for your organisation. As Kevin Simzer, CEO of Trend Micro and GM of North America region, said, the push to be innovative for customers is heightened as many companies move out of 'pandemic mode'. Paying close attention to closing the distance between an organisation and its customers also means addressing problems of security which are often associated with technological innovation. By security we mean ensuring that whatever connections are built in your ecosystem are perceived to be safe. For example, customers must trust that their data are secure, as Apple has promoted with its App Store and as Samsung has done with its Knox systems. Similarly, all connections established in the ecosystem must be securely guarded through either technological means or relational trustworthiness. We know that brand trust is paramount today, but the reality is that companies are only as innovative as they are secure. As businesses develop robust ecosystems to engage customers, trust means protecting and mitigating risk. For example, development operations teams take risks when developing new technologies, but they do not always consider the security implications. Being cutting-edge means successfully bridging the gaps between innovation, customer need and security. 'These are the core pillars of successful innovation in today's dynamic global marketplace', Simzer argues.

But while we consider connections as an important benefit of adopting RDHY, what might be the challenges for leaders and managers? If employees take total accountability for interactions with their customers, how do you engender trust, collaboration and cooperation within teams? And lastly, how do you build a positive employer brand? The answer to these lies in your ability to retain your good hands, because talent will shop around for the best offers and conditions of work. Such questions help you to reconsider the assumptions underpinning the traditional organisational hierarchy, so that everything now becomes refocused on supporting the customer as well as customer-facing teams, not to forget your own employees. A flatter organisational structure made up of empowered employees and interconnected teams is a much more effective model for leading the types of organisations that will win in the new economy. It fosters collaborative working, supplants individualism and supports a common purpose.

Business leaders have offered some thoughts on how to address leadership challenges in an ecosystem era. Anand Srivatsa, CEO, Tobii Tech, suggests:

> . . . innovations are only as strong as the team building them. Providing technology and solutions for customers that can have a significant impact on their business – and maybe even change the world – comes down to your employees and how you're empowering them. When leaders encourage their teams to think freely and creatively, they open up space to bring new ideas and technologies to the table. This long-standing commitment to pathfinding is starting to pay off as we see concepts like the metaverse emerge or technology like eye tracking being embedded into AR/VR devices. They help address some of the challenges that businesses' customers experience today, such as unnatural collaboration environments, while at the same time help bring to life some of the exciting technological advancements that have always been promised.

Operating with the RDHY approach frees up space for leaders and managers to focus on providing clear strategic direction and being a guiding light for self-organising teams. This also helps the teams to focus on driving innovation and improvement through deep customer interactions. Clearly therefore, in an ecosystem, you still need leadership – the world hasn't changed that much yet. However, the emphasis is on managers becoming enablers of ecosystem growth rather than mere enforcers of rules. As enablers, they are people who remove impediments, rather than create them through bureaucratic processes. The right attitude is not to shut down critical feedback and debate while remaining glued to ideologies which are no longer relevant for the time, but to expand your understanding and outlook and democratise decision-making. Hence, the key to successful leadership is striking a balance between alignment and empowerment. So, this is the ultimate goal: achieving a customer-focused, agile ecosystem comprising an interdependent and connected network of small teams, relentlessly pursuing increased customer value through rapid development cycles, unencumbered by hierarchy or bureaucracy and led by managers who promote a service culture through collaborative working and rewarding collective achievement.

Chapter summary, reflective questions and practical implications

Bear in mind that several changes may be taking place simultaneously which have implications for the decisions you will be making for your organisation. As the economic, legal or business landscapes change, the technological landscape is also evolving, and therefore what technology is able to do for you may change over time. The key thing is to keep a close watch and make adjustments as needed. In an ecosystem era, flexibility and being nimble are key. As a manager, developing some important competencies is key to your leadership within the ecosystem. For organisations, Haier provides an excellent example of how businesses can take advantage of opportunities, and adapt and thrive in a changing environment. Haier's success is due to its embrace of change and its willingness to cooperate with others in its business ecosystem. It has moved away from hierarchical modes of operation to a model that empowers everyone within the organisation. You, too, can deploy the lessons learnt in your own organisation.

Now that you know about the principles of RDHY, the belief systems underpinning it, and the triad – organisations, customers (users) and employees – we offer some questions to help you reflect on how you can apply your learning to your context. Remember, RDHY offers you the flexibility to make it yours, i.e. to adopt its principles in ways that work for your own business while keeping its core values of human-centricity. Think of the following:

- How might you look at your organisation differently in terms of the resources it has at the moment?
- As a manager, which of the 14 managerial competencies do you already have, and which ones must you develop?
- Is your organisation set up simply to enforce bureaucratic processes and rules, or to foster creativity and the spirit of entrepreneurship?
- What unique and unexplored opportunities exist for expanding your organisation into an ecosystem in your specific context?
- Are there opportunities that you may have missed in deepening your connection with your users?

- What investments in technology could you make that could develop and support the connections between your employees and users?

Bibliography

de Bono, E. (2009) *Lateral thinking: a textbook of creativity.* Penguin Books Limited.

Godley, A., Morawetz, N. & Soga, L. (2021) 'The complementarity perspective to the entrepreneurial ecosystem taxonomy', *Small Business Economics,* 56 (2): 723–738.

Haier. About Haier, available at https://www.haier.com/global/about-haier/intro/

Pereira, V., Temouri, K., Shen, N., Xie, X. & Tarba, S. (2022) 'Exploring multilevel innovative ecosystems and the strategies of EMNEs through disruptive global expansions – the case of a Chinese MNE', *Journal of Business Research,* 138: 92–107.

Reisinger, H. & Fetterer, D. (2021) 'Forget flexibility. Your employees want autonomy', *Harvard Business Review,* available at https://hbr.org/2021/10/forget-flexibility-your-employees-want-autonomy (accessed 19 August 2022).

Soga, L., Bolade-Ogunfodun, Y. & Laker, B. (2021) 'Design your work environment to manage unintended tech consequences', *MIT Sloan Management Review.*

Soga, L., Bolade-Ogunfodun, Y., Islam, N. & Amankwah-Amoah, J. (2022) 'Relational power is the new currency of hybrid work', *MIT Sloan Management Review.*

Soga, L., Laker, B., Bolade-Ogunfodun, Y. & Mariani, M. (2021) 'Embrace delegation as a skill to strengthen remote teams', *MIT Sloan Management Review,* 63 (1): 1–3.

Zhou, Y., Xian Jiaotong University & Haier Group (2017) 'Letter to the editor: Haier's Management Model of Rendanheyi: from Sea to Iceberg', *Management and Organization Review* 13(3): 687–688.

Part B

Strengthen

What factors affect the relationship between customers and employees? Dive deeper and put into action what RenDanHeYi is all about. Your organisation is nothing without your employees; it is also nothing without your customers. It is time to strengthen all loose ends in your RenDanHeYi triad.

Chapter 3

There are no employees without users

Introduction

One of the cornerstones of the RenDanHeYi (RDHY) philosophy is the central role occupied by users in the microenterprise while also upholding the centrality of the employee. This speaks to the conceptual understanding of the customer as a key factor in the birth, functioning and evolution of an ecosystem microcommunity (EMC) but also the employee as the driver of such an ecosystem. This is a bold approach to the notion of users who have typically been considered from an 'outside-in' perspective. The idea that there are no employees without customers suggests an intricate connectedness where one cannot exist without the other. This entwinement at the conceptual level also assumes an organisation without a boundary of who can be kept in and who is outside its walls.

This aligns with the advanced understanding of contemporary organisations and provides a critical backdrop for the RDHY model. The inextricable customer–employee relationship in this sense raises the bar for management practice as it does not have to think only about internal processes to make efficient gains, because what is internal is simultaneously open and impacts the external. The internal–external dichotomy is therefore challenged under the RDHY management model and we examine this idea more closely in this chapter. In particular, we show the symbiotic nature of the relationship and how it connects with the success of the EMC as the dynamic unit of the ecosystem.

Factors affecting the relationship between customers and employees

Customers and employees are integral parts of a larger network of relationships aimed at achieving several outcomes for organisational stakeholders. These relationships cut across regulatory agencies, the competitive market space, the supply chain, research and development bodies, organisational partnerships, and other strategic alliances. For the business organisation, the diverse nature of its stakeholder groups suggests that outcomes are also multifaceted, including both measurable and non-quantitative dimensions such as revenues, profitability, diversified product lines, satisfaction from consumption of produced goods and services, growth in market share and EMC expansion.

In typical capitalist work contexts, the employee–user relationship within this stakeholder space is often seen as purely transactional although designed to be complementary and mutually beneficial. While employees work towards providing services to the customer, the latter, in turn, pays for services rendered. Although this appears to be a straightforward exchange relationship, there are a number of interrelated factors that affect the relationship between employees and users. These include organisational structure, organisational goals and underlying assumptions about the relationship. These assumptions are expressed in the observable organisational culture in terms of espoused beliefs, values and practices, among others. For clarity, it may be useful to treat these two key actors sequentially. Beginning with the organisation, employees are typically seen as suppliers of labour and are rewarded for their labour through wages or other rewards systems which may include non-financial forms of remuneration.

For a critical stance, employees entering the organisation through traditional recruitment models are often seen as resources in the production function, that is, resources to be integrated with other resources such as land, raw materials or various forms of physical and financial capital. The overarching goal is usually determined by the business leader(s) within the context of a competitive market space and growth targets. Customers, on the other hand, tend to be seen as outside the formal boundaries of the organisation but integral to its continuity in the sense that they represent the object of organisational activities, and they hold valuable assets – financial resources which businesses need to continue operations. Business goals are shaped based on ideas of what would appeal to customers and what they would pay for. Businesses also often obtain feedback from customers in order to gauge the quality of their services and deploy different mechanisms to do so. This narrow view of the customer's relationship with the organisation suggests that decision-making and, indeed, power rest with the organisation while customers are simply recipients of the outcome of such decisions.

In terms of organisational structure, traditional business models have evolved from the classic bureaucratic structure, which is characterised by functional specialisation, hierarchy of authority, a system of rules, division of labour and impersonality. Contemporary forms of organising work have emerged, although features of bureaucratic organisational forms still exist. For example, your current organisation is likely to have policies, procedures and processes underpinning its activities. Simultaneously, more post-bureaucratic organisational forms leave room for discretionary decisions by employees in order to solve emerging problems. Underlying assumptions about power between employees, users and strategic partnerships also drive the relationships between customers and employees. Whereas in the more traditional forms of organising, formal power rests within the boundaries of the organisation, under the EMC model informal power lies with users, which places a huge premium on the relationship. As opposed to the traditional notion of a leader within an organisation making decisions that have an impact on users (who are deemed to be outside the organisation), the EMC model considers all members of the enterprise as the 'subject' of the enterprise. In other words, there is something of a balance of power, as EMC is driven by user needs which are then implemented by employees, yet the user is not 'king' *per se*, but rather a partner. (We will return to this idea of users or customers in greater depth in Chapter 4.)

RenDanHeYi in relation to employee roles

From the principles underpinning Talcott Parson's functionalism in sociology (see Bibliography), we tend to find ourselves playing various roles in our human sociality. The same holds in organisational life where every actor in the organisation must play their unique roles to ensure its successful running. This fundamental need is not erased with the deployment of RDHY but is strengthened in a way that simultaneously sustains other roles within the organisation. By organisation, we mean the newly conceptualised organisation that is boundaryless. The role of the employee is therefore intricately woven together with the role of the customer. The philosophy of RDHY assumes that the employee does not exist without the customer. In other words, there would be no functioning organisation if both the employee and the customer were not present. The absence of the customer is as much an existential threat to the organisation as the absence of the employee. For example, you could not have a bus driver without a bus and the network of supporting facilities that keep the bus on the road. This includes the road, the petrol station, passengers, traffic lights, bus stops, bus stations, etc. The absence of any of the elements that keep the bus on the road becomes an existential threat to being a bus driver. In other words, you would not exist without the assemblage of all the components that make you what or who you are. This idea is rooted in Latourian ontology of an actor–network in which the actor is not without the network of which he or she is a part. RDHY offers a similar understanding of the employee–customer relationship by acknowledging the uniqueness of each entity – customer or employee – while erasing the conceptual boundary that keeps one away from the other. As Figure 3.1 illustrates, RDHY dissolves the hard boundary of the organisation such that the users are drawn into a collaborative relationship with employees.

Rationally, employees remain employees and customers are customers, but the idea of the RDHY employee and the RDHY customer is one in which the customer is treated in the same way as the employee. For instance, you would need to support your employees in their roles in order to achieve employee satisfaction. You would often supply them (hopefully) with the needed resources, engage them in various ways, arrange relevant meetings, organise activities, etc. in order to get the best out of your employees in relation to their jobs. This is the same posture that must be taken in relation to the RDHY customer. That is, they need to be accorded similar courtesies and supported in their 'role' as customers in order to achieve customer satisfaction. They would also have the necessary resources supplied to them as part of their

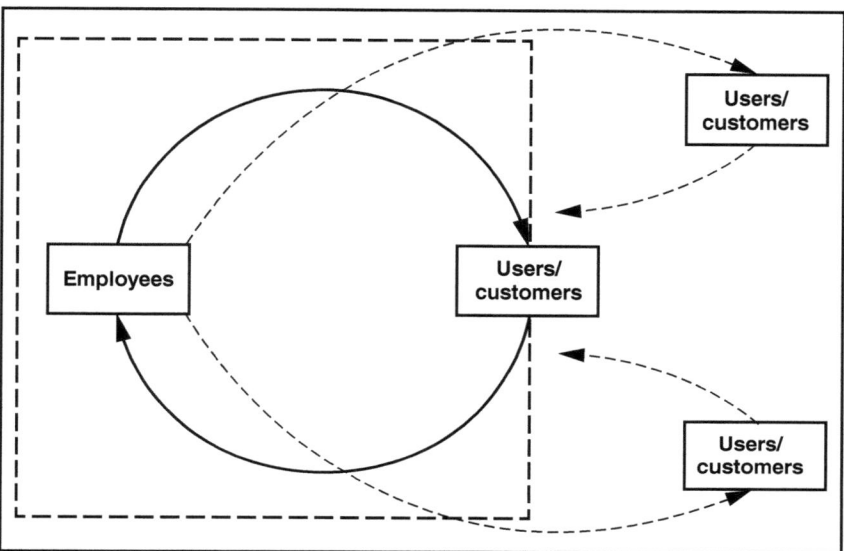

Figure 3.1 Connecting employees and users in the boundaryless RDHY organisation.

'membership' of the organisation; this might be informational resources or technical resources that ensure that the products they have purchased continue to function as they should. They would also be engaged with, at the least for customer feedback and suggestions, in order to get the best out of the customer now being a 'member' of the organisation. Equal weight is therefore placed on the organisation–employee and organisation–customer relationships, respectively. This conceptual clarity is needed to make RDHY operational within an organisation.

In the words of the British Sociologist, John Law: 'Napoleons are no different in kind to commoners.' The customer must not be treated any differently from the employee. They would be approached and understood as the employee, as both are needed for the survival of the RDHY organisation. This begs the question, is this not a truism that the customer and the employee are needed to make an organisation anyway? For a traditional organisation, the answer to this question is straightforward in theory. However, it is nuanced in practice. In the case of the former, managers would propound the importance of the customer, with the customer being 'king' (perhaps also 'queen', a rarely used term). The implication is that, the 'king' gets treated as king and the employee as the servant who must fulfil the wishes of the 'king'. The result is an organisation in which kings come from outside its gates to dictate to commoners within what they want. Failure to fulfil the desires of the 'king' often results in complaints, queries and compensations, but also frustrated workers who can't complain but have to suck it all up or risk losing their jobs. A quick chat with your local grocery store worker would offer you even deeper clarity than we could possibly capture on this page. Welcome to the service economy. But it doesn't have to be this way! In RDHY, both the customer and the employee are conceptualised differently. They are not in a king–servant relationship but are in partnership to deliver not just what the customer wants but what both believe will serve the customer's needs as they interact to produce a desired product for the customer. The result is a change in the traditional role of the employee. They are not there merely to serve the whims of a customer but to *work with* the customer as colleagues looking to deliver a product that fulfils a need. It is often said in project management that what a client wants is not necessarily what they need. The idea is to work with the client to ensure the project's benefits are realised. This couldn't be any truer for an RDHY customer–employee relationship; only in this instance there is no such thing as a 'project closeout' but a continuing relationship where all parties are interconnected (see Figure 2.2).

Employee skill set versus what customers want

Conventional Western management approaches to strategic staffing or resourcing in organisations is guided by the need to fit 'square pegs in square holes or round pegs in round holes'. This expression means that the right people are placed in the jobs that are appropriate for them. As a result, human resource management practices are designed to achieve this through a series of systematic processes. For many years, these have formed the bedrock of employee management principles and are still largely influential today. These processes include recruitment, selection, on-boarding and orientation, training and development, performance management and the design of remuneration or reward systems. The thinking underpinning this well-known model is that hiring people with the right skill sets ensures that an employee is fit for the job and can become productive. Some of these skills include communication, team working, leadership, and analytical and relationship management skills.

In the EMC model, a similar range of skills are valued; however, the entrepreneurial acumen is particularly prized. This organisational bent, though valuable under the EMC approach, presents challenges for employees who may not see themselves as being entrepreneurial. Indeed, evidence indicates that thousands of employee roles were made redundant at the early phase of establishing RDHY in Haier. Simultaneously, however, the focus on entrepreneurial skills also presents opportunities for flexibility and developing new skills for employees who embrace the challenge. The hiring policy within the EMC model is therefore based more on the idea of flexibility than on fit. In particular, the EMC model is open to new ideas from employees and offers them opportunities to initiate new microenterprises, by providing the needed platform support and resources. Under the RDHY philosophy, the users or customers provide the strategic input into product design for employees and are therefore critical to the continued existence of the EMC. However, and more critically, employees need to demonstrate entrepreneurship or intrapreneurship skills within the organisation in order to accurately respond to user needs. EMC leaders are particularly keen observers of users and their changing tastes and preferences. They have a fine-grained understanding of user demographics and a deep knowledge of their markets (and potential markets). In some cases, decisions are made to spin off other new EMCs from an existing one in order to better serve users. This work context suggests a dynamic yet integrated workflow where users see themselves as part of the EMC, although traditionally it could be said to exist outside of the formal organisation.

In the traditional conception of an organisation, the drive to meet key performance indicators (KPIs) could make employees focus on activities that meet the KPIs, irrespective of whether or not it satisfies the customer. This target-driven set of behaviours constitutes an expression of goal displacement and carries a risk of leading to friction between employees and customers. In contrast to conventional organisational structures, the RDHY model offers a more symbiotic relationship between employees and users. Through this relationship, it eliminates these potential friction points by shifting the power base to the users who primarily drive the activities and behaviours of employees. The philosophy of RDHY is not without its own KPIs; however, they are designed as customer-centric, and this structure provides impetus for employees to pursue their achievement (these KPIs are dealt with in greater detail in Chapter 8).

Additionally, the boundaries of a traditional organisation that keep its unique identity and separate it from its competition simultaneously create members and non-members. Whereas managers and employees remain as members of the traditional organisation, clients or customers become non-members. The customer is therefore not traditionally considered as a member of the organisation but as an outsider who patronises the organisation. RDHY challenges this implicit conceptualisation of the customer by removing the organisational boundary so that the customer and the employee see each other as belonging to one entity. The member/non-member friction is therefore erased in this sense. The EMC operates with open organisational boundaries involving partnerships, users and complementary providers who contribute to providing solutions for the customer.

Case Study 3.1 looks at Haier's implementation of RDHY following its acquisition of Japanese company Sanyo's refrigerator business in 2007 and its subsequent takeover of Sanyo's entire white goods business five years later. The understanding that there are no users without entrepreneurs and vice-versa meant that Haier needed a highly motivated workforce that was ready to engage with customers in an intimate way as part of the philosophical underpinnings of RDHY, which also runs counter to what was being practised for several years in the acquired company. When Haier acquired Sanyo's refrigerator business in 2007, 70% of Sanyo's employees were over 50 years old. The Business Department director at that time was 59, and there were four or five people at the lower level who were 57 or 58, all waiting to be promoted to replace the director. Employee performance was not of concern but to muddle along until it was your turn to be promoted. Haier decided to bring in young employees with an average age of 25 who would change the status quo. These young employees were tasked with

Case Study 3.1

Haier's acquisition of Sanyo in Japan

Twenty years after tapping into the Japanese market, Haier built a factory and two R&D centres in Japan and now run two sales companies in this regional market where they have integrated their production, sales and R&D efforts. Hiring about 700 Japanese employees in Japan, Haier faced an enormous responsibility for the entire process from product development to after-sales services while also ensuring that customers are won over to the brand. After moving into the Japanese market in 2002, the company acquired Sanyo's refrigerator business in 2007, and took over Sanyo's entire white goods business in 2012. This journey in Japan went from independent development to acquisitions and then back again to independent development of Haier's own products.

Haier's organisational culture was very different from that of Sanyo, which is a Japanese company. The difference was perhaps a reflection of the traditional bureaucratic organisation structure of Japanese society that is also evident in most workplaces. For example, Sanyo's recruitment method, seniority-based system and lifetime employment model all pointed to a highly bureaucratic process with several levels of managerial approval. By contrast, Haier had been implementing some organisational change processes, including transforming functional departments into supporting platforms, and turning leaders into resource providers, thus establishing an inverted-pyramid organisational structure, in which every employee was encouraged to be customer-facing in their work routines. Having that same impact within the newly acquired Sanyo in order to subsume its culture into Haier's was a major challenge. More importantly, it was increasingly clear that a Chinese brand in a Japanese society could only gain customer loyalty if the company took steps to bring employees and customers together by breaking the hierarchical connection between these two entities.

Haier soon realised that implementing RDHY was crucial in order to achieve a user-driven organisational structure that the

> model propounds. It is worth noting that in the early stages of Japan's economic development, seniority-based systems and lifetime employment played an important role. These traditional approaches constituted an operational model that survived for generations and is highly regarded in Japan. However, the changes of times and market competition exposed many drawbacks of this model. One example of such shortcomings is that it created a workforce that wanted remuneration based on seniority and position and not productivity; a worker only had to wait to be a senior in order to be promoted. As a result, the seniority-based system stifled creativity and innovation for entry-level employees as they found it difficult to break the artificial boundaries of age and seniority to showcase their creativity. Haier needed that younger workforce for its transformational objectives.

a shared vision of leading performance targets and efficiency and their remuneration would now be driven by these metrics instead of seniority. A slow, bottom-up approach began to turn the tide for the waning Sanyo (now Haier) as these younger employees began to drive growth by focusing on the customer, establishing relationships and deploying the principles of RDHY to ensure that the voice of the customer was heard and their needs met in order to deliver on their performance objectives. Mr Kubota, who was in charge of Sanyo's Japanese research and development (R&D) department, commented on the company's previous performance and said, 'We were developing products according to the instructions of our director, and the resulting product needed to meet the requirements given to me. The negative growth was attributed to the sales department and had nothing to do with me.'

Before the merger and acquisition, the R&D department had been in deficit for 10 years and the man in charge denied any responsibility for this failure. The department failed to see its primary responsibility as being linked to the users to whom they needed to create and deliver value. Implementing RDHY therefore needed to permeate every aspect of the organisation. The attitudes of workers needed to be challenged and the transformation was needed in every department. Implementing RDHY was not simply putting a concept into practice but a complete remodelling of the organisation. In Japan, the hook was to change the remuneration system from seniority and position to performance target. Specifically, Haier turned Sanyo's original salary arrangement of 12-month salaries plus 4 months of bonuses to one of 12-month salaries plus uncapped bonuses. This reform meant that apart from the guaranteed minimum income, employees' potential overall income could increase significantly. This is not an egalitarian approach but a performance-based process that rewards employees for what they have done and not how long they have been with the company or what position they hold. These strategies provided some form of further motivation for younger employees who wanted to showcase their abilities while also being rewarded for their efforts.

In achieving high performance, employees embraced the RDHY principle of bringing the customer closer in order to understand his or her needs and deliver value. To achieve this task, the role of technology was necessary. Initially, the technology was considered as a means by which employees could engage with customers. Subsequently, the technology became a platform where both employees and customers began to exchange ideas in ways that brought the customer closer than originally anticipated. The implementation of RDHY was now beginning to take root as the door between customers and employees remained open.

Haier Group's acquisition of Sanyo was its first overseas project. At that time, Chinese companies had just started their drive to acquire overseas businesses. It was unusual for Haier, a household appliances company from a developing country, to acquire a Japanese Fortune 500 company that was in decline. Predictions of market success were not in Haier's favour, but its RDHY model of management changed the game, and today Haier is a success story in Japan.

Practical steps to deepen the relationship with technology

The human–technology relationship has always remained an elusive one. While we (perhaps ignorantly) think we know who the human is (at least for now), our limited understanding of our own creations – in this case, technology – continues to expose our inability as humans to make sense of our relationships. The RDHY management philosophy shapes our relationship with technology in another light. As explained earlier (in Chapter 2), connecting technologies are actors in the triad of the organisation, the employee and the customer, serving almost as the glue that holds all three elements together. In essence, what holds all three together is the human-centricity of RDHY, but in practice, technology facilitates the bringing together of all RDHY actors.

Case Study 3.1 looking at Haier Japan showed the deployment of technology that facilitated employee–customer relations. One may be tempted to assume that technology is what is driving the relationship, especially as the organisation is now a porous (actually boundaryless) entity and therefore something must serve as a connecting thread that holds it all together, as the organisation could not possibly exist metaphorically as the open sea. Technology therefore plays a key role in the RDHY organisation, except that it is not simply a tool that is used to bring customers and employees together but is a platform or a space in which all parties engage. In other words, the instrumental view of technology does not hold and, therefore, how we build a new relationship with technology becomes the question of concern.

The connecting technologies participating in the RDHY organisation are, in this sense, participants as are the other parties involved. As a platform where all RDHY actors engage, the technology is implicitly bestowed the status of a place, although it is a non-place. For example, 'I am going to the office for work' assumes that the office is a place to which the individual goes to do some activity. This individual would have to live in that office space and take advantage of all that the office allows them to do so that they can fulfil their work activities. Similarly, the participating technologies in an RDHY organisation could be considered as 'spaces' that bring together customers and employees. To deepen one's engagement in this space, the individual must choose to 'go to' that place in order to engage. The technology must therefore be a friendly place to which all members can go. Research in the late 1980s by Fred Davies showed that individuals would accept a technology if they deemed it as user-friendly. A practical guide to deepening the relationship with technology is therefore to:

- *Make the technology as welcoming a place as possible to allow all RDHY parties to engage without inhibitions.* You can do this by ensuring the technology is user-friendly. This might mean working closely with developers (where possible) to ensure the user interface is simple and visually welcoming. We recently worked with a Fortune 500 organisation that contacted Google to help improve the user experience of Google Currents, a Google-owned platform for corporate communication and team collaboration.

- *Consider, where necessary, (re)designing your own technology for improved intuitiveness.* Although there are several off-the-shelf technologies you could adopt, you might want to have something more bespoke to serve your unique needs. In fact, this can sometimes be a matter of branding where you wish to run your own generic technologies. Take, for instance, Walgreens Boots Alliance which runs its own Pharmacy Unscripted® platform for internal corporate communications.

- *Develop a system for regular updates in order to prevent any potential hiccups.* Always assume that whatever technology you use is in a state of perpetual beta. In other words, your technology platform is not a once-and-for-all software application that can be left unattended to. Adversarial attacks on technology can often be foiled or prevented through updates to software.

- *Be open to innovative technologies that are not 'intra' focused, like legacy intranets, but are outward-facing to ensure that your RDHY organisation remains truly open to its members.* At the same time, ensure that the necessary encryption techniques are in place in order to build confidence in the use of the technology. This means paying attention to security issues to ensure that all users on your technology platforms are protected from cyber-attacks and that information shared across the platforms is secure.

- *Give users of the technology as many 'admin rights' as possible.* They should be able to change settings that matter to them. This ensures that they feel trusted in their use of the technology and engage with other users in ways that are meaningful and trustworthy.

The dangers of not connecting the employees and users

Research within the field of strategic management in general, and marketing in particular, is often associated with a customer-centric approach to running a business, as the customer is believed to hold the key to predictable streams of revenue and, therefore, sustainable business models. Strategic marketing scholar Stan Maklan's 2011 article, 'Why CRM [customer relationship management] fails and how to fix it' as well as a more recent work by Gene Cornfield in 2021, entitled 'Recognizing your customer's purpose is key to growth', have shown that the relationship between the customer and employees is significant for identifying customer pain points, understanding customer needs, segmenting the market, targeting particular groups and positioning the brand of the organisation. In other words, employees serve as an important filter for distilling user needs. Employees are particularly important for transmitting the needs and desires of the users into actionable responses and solutions that aim to meet those needs. It goes without saying that employees may inadvertently also allow for leakages within this information flow. Such leakages constitute lost opportunities for new business. The EMC model attempts to capture such leakages by building a watertight relationship between users and employees, based on the RDHY philosophy as well as other factors such as shared goals, shared income, distributed leadership, potential for increased revenues and growth via other related spin-offs. Thus, where there is a disconnect between end users and employees, there is a lost sense of direction as far as understanding evolving employee needs is concerned and a waste of scarce resources. This leaves the business open to competitive rivalry, which may cost it its market share.

Renowned professor Ron Adner's recent article in 2021, 'Sharing value for ecosystem success', suggests that the traditional ego-centred approach is no longer viable and the direction to take is to have an ecosystem approach that allows value-sharing across stakeholders. This is in stark contrast to conventional structures which revolve around the company alone. Where a company is positioned at the centre of an ecosystem which is seen as revolving around it, there are likely to be constraints to growth potential. To solidify the connection between employees and users, therefore, there is value in expanding the power base to include customers as key stakeholders who bring value to the organisation. They provide value not just in terms of revealing current needs but also in terms of signalling changing and future needs. This information then forms the strategic basis on which the organisation responds with products which are tailored to meet user needs across a range of markets. In this way, both users and employees are working to advance the other's interests.

There are studies on managing customer relationships and these emphasise the need to have a service philosophy, create the right organisational structure and an information management system which keeps a business in tune with its customers' dynamic needs. These include work by management scholar George Day in 2003, entitled 'Creating a superior customer-relating capability', and Stan Maklan's 2011 article on ensuring CRM success. However, it is important to address the employee dimension as critical to creating satisfied customers. Despite huge expenditure on customer relationship marketing, Stan Maklan, who researches customer relationship management, argues that a positive employee experience contributes to developing additional value for a business. In this light, the RDHY model speaks to the aspects of empowerment, autonomy and creativity that many employees tend to welcome in their roles. By offering opportunities for greater ownership, closer engagement with customers, new business idea generation and supporting the creation of microenterprises, employees are provided with both financial and non-financial forms of motivation. This allows them to achieve their goals of meeting and exceeding user needs while also meeting their organisational growth targets.

Ideas to engage customers and employees immediately

We have found that engaging customers and employees is no longer an option. In a highly competitive market where customers are increasingly vocal, ignoring them or merely listening to them is not what RDHY suggests. The key is to engage the customer and, beyond that, to bring the customer into the organisation.

We offer a few tips on how to do this:

- *Redefine the roles of your employees.* You can do this by specifying a customer-facing element as part of the measure of performance, including the extent to which the employee has interacted with these new members of the organisation, either directly or indirectly.
- *Go beyond using social media to respond to customers to using it to relate with customers.* This means you should proactively engage and communicate with your customers rather than waiting for queries or complaints to come in before you respond to these. For example, being proactive in relating with your customers could involve sending updates of your company's current performance as soon as they are available, sharing your growth plans, signalling new areas of business you want to launch into, as well as your recent achievements. In this way, customers get to have a sense of belonging as they would be well informed about developments in your business.
- *Shift your organisational orientation of the customer as an outsider to that of an insider.* You can run regular training programmes for your employees to share the new vision and its implication for your business. This helps you to obtain the buy-in of your employees and allows for truly open organisational boundaries, which facilitate value-sharing across all stakeholders in a symbiotic and mutually beneficial relationship.
- *Organise customer hackathons to keep communication lines open and generate innovative ideas.* Also issue rewards accordingly, as these reward systems signal that their loyalty is valued.
- *Invite customer groups into your company to physically engage with employees.* Make a big splash of this and let the ecosystem know. Identify lead users and turn them into champions for your brand. They will tell their own story to the world as effective ambassadors. It is not only influencers who can help to sell; your customers will have a more sustained impact than one influencer. You are not after sales alone; you are after relationship-building.

Chapter summary, reflective questions and practical implications

In this chapter, we present RDHY's radical approach to elevating customers (or end users) as powerful stakeholders within the business ecosystem and its positioning of them as insiders, rather than outsiders. As a result, the insider–outsider dichotomy is challenged as employees and customers are brought together through RDHY. Consequently, we highlight the unconventional view of users as occupying a similar leadership status to employees in a microenterprise.

- As 'leaders', customers are directly linked to the formation, structure and evolution of EMCs as a result of their role in providing critical data points needed for strategic decision-making. We use the word 'leaders' carefully so as not to create the idea of other elements of the ecosystem being 'followers'. On the contrary, we use 'leaders' to demonstrate the availability of an environment that allows or encourages the agency of the customer. The EMC therefore grows in direct response to an understanding of user needs as they evolve. In other words, there is a shared understanding of the purpose of the EMC as existing to serve users while simultaneously making them aware of the role of the enterprise in meeting their needs.

- The voice of the customer is prominent and is reflected in the strategic decisions made by the EMC in terms of partnerships that produce solutions for the customer or decisions that expand and spin off other EMCs. This inherent propensity to expand in potentially unlimited ways is what drives the formation of the ecosystem and, more recently, the Internet of Things.

- To ensure sustained productivity, focus on directly fulfilling the needs of your customers as you would your employees. Deploy whatever resource will help you to achieve this, including the strategic use of technology to facilitate the interconnectedness between employees and customers. An RDHY-practising organisation is therefore one that understands that, really, there can be no employee without a customer and that takes steps to ensure the centrality of both in its practice of management.

Bibliography

Adner, R. (2021) 'Sharing value for ecosystem success', *MIT Sloan Management Review*, available at https://sloanreview.mit.edu/article/sharing-value-for-ecosystem-success/ (accessed 14 November 2022).

Callon, M. (1986) 'Some elements of a sociology of translation: domestication of the scallops and the fishermen of St Brieuc Bay', in J. Law (ed.) *Power, action and belief*. London: Routledge, pp. 196–233.

Callon, M. (1987) 'Society in the making: the study of technology as a tool for sociological analysis', in Bijker, W. E., Hughes, T. P., & Pinch, T. J. (eds) *The social construction of technological systems: New directions in the sociology and history of technology*. Cambridge, MA: MIT Press, pp. 83–103.

Callon, M. (1991) 'Techno-economic networks and irreversibility', in Law, J. (ed.) *A sociology of monsters: essays on power, technology and domination*. London: Routledge, pp. 132–161.

Cornfield, G. (2021) 'Recognizing your customer's purpose is key to growth', *Harvard Business Review*, available at https://hbr.org/2021/05/whats-your-customers-purpose (accessed 14 November 2022).

Davis, F. D. (1989) 'Perceived usefulness, perceived ease of use, and user acceptance of information technology', *MIS Quarterly*, 13(3): 319–340.

Day, G. S. (2003) 'Creating a superior customer-relating capability', *MIT Sloan Management Review*, available at https://sloanreview.mit.edu/article/creating-a-superior-customerrelating-capability/ (accessed 14 November 2022).

Latour, B. (1986b) 'Visualisation and cognition: Drawing things together', in Kuklick, H. (ed.) *Knowledge and society: studies in the sociology of culture past and present*. Greenwich, CT: JAI Press, pp. 1–40.

Latour, B. (1996) 'On interobjectivity', *Mind, Culture, and Activity*, 3(4), 228–245.

Latour, B. (2005) *Reassembling the social: an introduction to actor-network Theory*. Oxford: Oxford University Press.

Law, J. (1992) 'Notes on the theory of the actor-network: ordering, strategy, and heterogeneity', *Systems Practice*, 5(4), 379–393.

Maklan, S., Knox, S. & Peppard, J. (2011) 'Why CRM fails and how to fix it', *MIT Sloan Management Review*, available at https://sloanreview.mit.edu/article/why-crm-and-how-to-fix-it/ (accessed 14 November 2022).

Parsons, T. (1937) *The structure of social action*. New York, NY: The Free Press.

Parsons, T. (1971) *The system of modern societies*. Englewood Cliffs, NJ: Prentice-Hall (Foundations of Modern Sociology Series).

Parsons, T. & Shils, E. A. (2001) *Toward a general theory of action: theoretical foundations for the social sciences* (1st ed.). New York, NY: Routledge.

How to engage the distracted customer

Introduction

This chapter explores the connection between the organisation and the customer. With insights from spectacular leaders in renowned organisations, we consider the different perspectives that corporate boards and senior leaders have on their customers, both philosophically and concerning data. We give direction on the technology required to understand customer viewpoints, particularly in a world of customer disloyalty and competition for attention and use real evidence to show that customer satisfaction – not investor satisfaction – can make or break a business. We also offer reflective questions to prompt you to develop your understanding of the customer and the customer–organisation connection.

The customer–organisation connection

We previously established the customer as integral to the continued existence of your business organisation (see Chapter 3). More importantly, from a business ecosystem perspective, we demonstrated why ecosystem micro-communities (EMCs) are expressions of a service culture that elevates the customer to an equal stakeholder position as employees, a radical approach to conceptions of the customer as user. In this new paradigm, the relationship with users is imperative for business continuity. In Alvin Toffler's neologism of the prosumer, he conceived of the customer as one who is deeply involved in the organisation. He predicted the end of an era where the manufacturer of a product was the only one who had a say in what the market should buy. We began to realise Toffler's prediction in the era of IKEA where customers were involved in producing what they wanted by assembling it themselves, but this did not quite fulfil the import of what Toffler meant. Motorola, with its Moto Maker, also allowed customers to customise their own products with a range of choices to be made. This approach gained popular acclaim but could not be sustained, nor did it realise Toffler's dream of the prosumer.

At its radical core, RenDanHeYi (RDHY) fulfils Toffler's vision of the future as the customer is there not only to customise a product but also to belong to the organisation. This approach to management challenges organisational boundaries and creates an ecosystem that operates like a living organism with many functioning parts that are distinct in and of themselves. The connection between the customer and the organisation is one that empowers the customer, who is now considered as an organisational member and not an outsider looking simply to customise products. It calls for a different kind of engagement. This engagement is different from the customer waking up in the morning like an employee and thinking about the organisation or getting ready to come to the office. It is not an engagement where the customer is happy to exchange email conversations with you as organisational members would do. It is also not an engagement involving key performance indicators (KPIs) that the customer must meet in order to remain part of the organisation. In fact, it would be foolhardy to think that RDHY asserts a customer connection without the contextual understanding that the customer has other companies they deal with. They are perhaps customers of your competitor organisations and potentially have more brand allegiance to other companies. This understanding is necessary in order not to assume a robotic RDHY connection of customers to your company. This is simply not tenable. The customer is free to engage with other companies. He or she may perhaps be unwilling to have any connection with your company for their own personal reasons and they must be accorded that space to make their own decision. The philosophical underpinnings of RDHY acknowledge the agency of the human and this is no different in how the customer is conceptualised and related to.

Establishing a connection between the customer and the organisation also takes into account the customer experience. Chief Digital Officer at J.D. Power Bernado Rodriguez[1] suggests that customer experience can be adversely impacted when customers' only point of connection with the organisation is through digital platforms. Consequently, if your organisation's main interaction with customers is through digital platforms, you may have a situation in which the customer has little affinity towards your organisation as there is potentially a good degree of digital platform homogeneity across your sector. You don't want to let digital fatigue draw your customer away from your organisation, although some thoughtfulness about what platforms to use becomes necessary. In fact, this is because a focus on the technology can offer some benefits, although it may do little to create any new value, as some studies[2] have warned. The connection between the customer and the organisation must therefore be at the core of the organisation deploying RDHY and the customer experience can set the stage for the success or failure of any customer–organisation relationship. This means we must seek out what customers value.

You may believe your company captures, creates and delivers value to your customers, but do we know what they value? It is not what we think they value but what they truly value that we need to understand if any connection with customers will work. More importantly, can you measure that value? Although the management model of RDHY is highly human-centric, we find in our research that organisations practising RDHY do not necessarily work without quantitative measures. Peter Drucker's supposed saying of 'what gets measured gets managed' arguably runs through the management practices of an RDHY organisation, although qualitative and contextual factors are given equal value.

Measuring what the customer values is therefore of paramount importance to establishing a connection with the customer. This is first done by understanding the needs of the customer. It requires patient engagement with the customer in order to understand what their pain points are. It means deciphering what the customer needs versus what they want. Eliciting customer needs is therefore at the core of establishing an organisation–customer connection. This is a qualitative activity which seeks to explore the customer's context and sometimes hidden factors that would impact the customer–organisation relationship. For example, a customer might want a fully connected Internet of Things (IoT) kitchen installed but the contextual elements like network connectivity might hinder the full functionality of such an installation. In that regard, an RDHY organisation would not merely seek to install what the customer 'wants' when it is evident that the full benefits of the product may not be realised by the customer. In this case, the customer might be advised to consider other options that deliver solutions to the customer's needs, such as standalone devices for instance. This human-centricity of RDHY in management practice allows the organisation to connect at a deeper level with the customer. The relationship is therefore one that is collaborative and mutually beneficial, not exploitative or solely profit-oriented. Customers are not naive. They can see if or when an organisation is only after the bottom line. They can also see through the double standards that some organisations demonstrate, and they can tell whether an organisation is genuinely interested in them or just looking for a sale. As a result, an RDHY organisation is one that places people before profit and that values the customer relationship as the bloodline of the organisation. In this way, the customer connects to the values of the organisation and is not a distant entity.

It was Simon Sinek who popularly argued that customers buy the 'why' of an organisation and not the 'what'. This thinking holds some value when it comes to the underpinning philosophy of an RDHY organisation. The values of the organisation are carried along in the day-to-day operations so that, in connecting with customers, there is transmission of those values, and the customer feels that deeper connection for a zero-distance relationship.

How corporate boards and senior leaders see users

The importance of the senior leadership of any organisation to its connection with customers cannot be overestimated. This is particularly the case in the digital era where a tweet from a senior leader has the potential to cause significant ripple effects in how the organisation is perceived, as well as its market capitalisation. For example, a series of tweets[3] by Elon Musk in May 2020 wiped nearly $15 billion off electric car company Tesla's market capitalisation. This also led to a personal loss of $3 billion from his own stock in the company. Two years previously, Musk triggered an investigation into his company's market moving operations through what looked like a mundane tweet, but one that also led to a $20 million fine. Later, in November 2021, Musk decided to engage with customers on Twitter through a poll to determine whether he should sell 10% of his stock in order to pay more taxes. This was an unprecedented move by any CEO of a large and influential company on many accounts. First, Musk won the admiration of many in the Twittersphere for his transparency in engaging customers, or rather his followers, on a subject that he could have made a sole decision on. Second, it was admirable, perhaps altruistic, to ask people whether they would agree to him giving away more in taxes. The answer was obvious. Third, the art of seeking the opinion of customers or followers for such an important decision carried within it some element of a customer connection, or at least a follower connection. Fourth, Musk was no novice to the impact of his Twitter activity on his company but chose to make this move anyway. Perhaps he imagined this 'good' approach of asking people to decide on doing something 'good', such as paying more taxes, might enhance his own reputation and that of the company's with subsequent positive effects on the company's value. If this latter assumption was the driving force for Musk's actions, the result turned out to be quite the opposite.[4] *Fortune* magazine reported how the company lost more than $200 billion in market value after Musk posted his tweet about paying more tax. This also cost him a 15% loss in personal fortune.

We observe that senior leadership's connection with customers has its place but can also go terribly wrong if the perspectives held about that customer relationship are not well aligned. In the case of Musk, we see a senior leader engaging with customers as 'followers'. This perspective is not necessarily a bad thing. In fact, a senior leader is able to use strategies that spur on followership to take some actions that benefit the leader. We have seen political leaders amass a large following on Twitter as they galvanise people to take various actions. In remarkable yet unprecedented fashion, we have seen the likes of Donald Trump, a former US President, banned indefinitely from Twitter and suspended from Facebook in 2021 as a result of what was considered repugnant platform behaviours. Other influential figures have used online platforms to raise funds for charity, while others engage people for various good causes like climate change. We discuss the value of participating technologies in Chapter 6. What is important here is this perspective of the 'customer as follower' triggering these kinds of engagements that are akin to various activities in the Twittersphere and social media in general. For an RDHY organisation, this perspective of the 'customer as follower' is antithetical to what RDHY stands for. The customer as follower assumes a following in any direction towards which senior leaders drive customers. It creates Napoleons and commoners. This conceptualisation engenders a class system in which customers are hopelessly unable to fulfil their needs unless the organisation provides the solutions. This approach is one in which the organisation makes a product and expects the customer to buy it. Within such organisations, employees are pushed to make sales and the focus is often the bottom line. This kind of perspective also means that huge amounts of money are spent on advertisements in order to convince 'followers', and the so-called market research agenda is often to identify where products can be pushed to. At its extreme, this perspective holds in various 'Ponzi' schemes so that the greater the number of followers, the better it is for business.

There may be benefits to the customer-as-follower perspective. For instance, if you wish to start a revolution with a product that tackles climate change, you will want to have your customers committed to following your steps in every way so that you can gain momentum. Beware, however, that a 'following' does not necessarily equate to a long-term relationship. Followers might identify with another cause or organisation and leave you. Leadership scholar Joseph Rost[5] warned that this whole idea of followers is a hopeless and irredeemable one. People are not sheep. In a post-industrial age, people must be considered as collaborators and not mere followers, Rost argues. This idea runs through followership theories in leadership studies. In fact, follower-centric approaches to leadership uniformly eschew all conceptualisations of people as simply there to passively partake in a leadership relationship. Unfortunately, the use of the word follower remains obdurate in leadership theories and continues to carry a religious connotation even though theorising around the idea of the follower has accorded it agency in the leadership relationship. The customer-as-follower perspective is therefore also philosophically at odds with followership theories of leadership. The follower has agency and can exercise it as they please.

Another perspective of the customer is one that holds the customer as king. This marketing cliché of the customer being king evolved from Harry Selfridge, who is credited to saying at the turn of the twentieth century that 'the customer is always right'. If there was any doubt or misgivings, Selfridges as a successful luxury shopping brand could be considered a vindication for Harry Selfridge's mantra which accentuated the importance of the customer and, of course, future customers. Later in the mid-twentieth century, advertising chief David Ogilvy, who warned against what seemed to be a hyperbolic presentation of the customer in advertising campaigns, declared, 'The customer is not a moron. She's your wife'. Surely, this advice was well received, as Jack Mitchell, CEO of Mitchells/Richards, luxury clothing retailers based in Connecticut, USA, emphasised the importance of hugging your customers. Yes, that includes physical hugging, literally, but also metaphorically or both. Mitchell attributes the success of his family business empire to that strong customer-centric approach so that even through difficult economic downturns, the company excelled as they kept hugging their customers. Again, the success of Mitchell's business empire could be seen as vindication of such positioning of the customer as indeed king, who deserves worship, or perhaps a wife who deserves hugs. We want to believe that Mitchell's ideas, which he expressed in 2003, and those of Ogilvy in 1955 were also intended to be somewhat humorous, although they seriously considered them as necessary ingredients for running successful businesses. These mantras have become embedded in management practice, with several business training sessions conducted to show techniques of how to please the customer who is king.

Training Magazine's industry report[6] has tracked corporate training expenditure annually in the United States since 1981 and has found an overall increase, with $83 billion spent in 2019 alone. Between 2014 and 2019, the least expenditure in a year on corporate training programmes was $61.8 billion with a high of $87 billion recorded in 2018. From our own research on Haier's conglomerate, we believe this large deployment of resources for employee training programmes, with key elements targeted at customer satisfaction, are inadequate. More radically, *Forbes* contributor Dan Pontefract calls these training programmes a waste.[7] In our view, the mantra of the customer as king, or perhaps as wife, that underpins many of these training programmes is itself flawed. The idea that the customer is king creates a power imbalance which results in its abuse, as absolute power corrupts absolutely. This results in scenarios in which customers feel privileged and become overly expectant of unrealistic service delivery from employees. In some cases, employees are abused by customers, and senior leaders, who are often not on the ground, pile on the pressure in an almost Draconian style for employees to deliver customer satisfaction. This customer relationship perspective results in senior leaders being detached from their employees, as they only look to metrics of customer satisfaction. It spirals into a never-ending cycle in which the customer king wants more, the senior leader as the king's warden pushes for more, and the employee is left with no other choice than either to follow suit or leave the organisation, dejected. This management approach focuses mainly on the numbers and not on the human, in contrast to the management philosophy of RDHY.

The message is clear, which is that all these customer perspectives, although holding good intentions of improving customer service, trigger unintended consequences of dehumanising the personhood of employees. In the case of the customer as follower, it is the customer who is dehumanised, more like a sheep following its shepherd. RDHY therefore offers a way out of this management conundrum by putting the human back into the organisation. It emphasises the value of the human, be it customer or employee, and creates conditions that remove any power imbalance, thus allowing the customer and the employee to relate on an equal footing.

The role of technology in a world of customer disloyalty and competition

The technological terrain has experienced rapid shifts globally as we move from the computer age to the age of digital intelligence. In this era, data is the new gold rush and organisations deploy various technologies to harvest data about customers, often surreptitiously. These range from the use of online adverts to website cookies, but also include direct data-harvesting activities that are done with algorithms running stealthily without the customer's knowledge. These ideas have crept into the mobile apps domain as mobile commerce sales[8] soar, almost quadrupling from 2016 to 2021. These increasing activities of data harvesting through mobile apps have led to Apple and Google, two of the largest app store hosts, offering users greater control over what data they allow apps to collect on customer usage. Nonetheless, with ever advancing algorithmic tools, data continues to be collected on customer usage as individuals leave data footprints about their online activities. The assumption is that the organisation who knows more about customer behaviours can tailor that information to beat the competition. Consequently, organisations recruit data scientists and consultancy groups with expertise in customer data crunching to ensure they are ahead of the game.[9] Research by Glassdoor's economic research team in 2019 reported by Forbes and Bloomberg found that the highest entry-level paying jobs in the United States are those of data scientists at $95,000, closely followed by software engineering jobs at $90,000. International Data Corporation (IDC)[10] predicted global spending on big data and analytics solutions to reach $215.7 billion in 2021, which is 10.1% higher than what the spending was in 2020.

This dependence on data has thus led to organisations channelling resources to harvesting and analysing customer data to the disadvantage of developing strategies that yield real customer connection. The global customer experience management market was valued at over $7.5 billion in 2020 and predicted to increase at an annual compound growth rate of 17.5% for the next eight years. According to Grand View Research's market analysis report,[11] this growing importance of understanding customer activity has contributed to a growth in customer experience management systems. There is much to learn from customer data but that alone does not necessarily offer value when it comes to organisation–customer connection in the digital era. This is because there are competing spectacles for the customer, and dependence on their digital footprints only remotely connects the organisation without eliciting any added value. The focus on customer data analysis stems from an attention to the bottom line as it sees the customer as a quantifiable unit that can be translated into monetary benefits. This does not augur well for establishing a customer relationship.

To build a strong customer relationship, it is important that senior leaders take necessary steps to understand customer viewpoints.

In other words, managers must seek to see through the lens of the customer in order to understand what drivers to pursue for staying ahead. The design company IDEO has a well-established approach that puts the human experience at the centre of product design. This is referred to as design thinking and its goal is to seek to understand what customers need, not what our collective experience or capacity believes customers want. There are elements of RDHY in operation, as IDEO's main approach is a human-centred design. It is not a process that depends on online data harvesting but one that looks for real-life customer experiences. It engages primary data, working directly with customers in order to create, capture and deliver value for customers. In 2010, IDEO launched a collaborative platform called OpenIDEO which allowed the company's designers to work closely with customers. This technological platform continues to serve as an open door and a space where both customers and designers can interact and work together towards a solution that meets the customer's needs. OpenIDEO thus ensures a cross-fertilisation of ideas among a team of people with varying expertise as well as the customer. The process establishes a collaborative environment with a great customer relationship and its end ensures the customer's needs are fully met. This example shows an engagement of the customer in the very process of product design, thus boosting confidence in the customer and creating loyalty to the organisation as they feel involved.

Just like OpenIDEO, organisations that practise RDHY involve the customer in similar fashion. The customer becomes almost indistinguishable from the employee as both parties are intricately involved in the process of value creation. Leaders in an RDHY organisation seek to work with the customer to deliver value, not to raise share prices for investors. As it turns out, the zero-distance approach between the organisation and the customer ultimately means that the shareholders are themselves also organisational members; therefore, creating value for customers is, by default, creating value for shareholders. As highlighted in an earlier chapter, the management practice of RDHY operates within an ecosystem with several interconnected actors working together as one complete whole. Accordingly, the bifurcation between leaders and shareholders as seen in non-RDHY organisations does not exist. The implication is that it is not investor pressure that drives organisational outcomes but customer needs, as the organisation works closely with its valued members who, in this case, are the customers.

Although we acknowledge that data analytics has its place in targeting customers, our contention is that it does not meet the human-centric approach that RDHY stands for. As a result, technologies that are needed for capturing 'customer data' in an RDHY organisation are not those that are distant from the customer or those that stealthily obtain data about the customer. Instead, they are technologies that engage the customer so that the customer feels involved without being an external party to the organisation. As we argued earlier, this involvement of the customer is what builds customer loyalty. It makes it easier for the customer to sieve out the demands for attention from other competing companies or brands.[12] Research from Wharton School's *Marketing Metrics* shows it is up to 14 times more likely to sell a product to a loyal customer than to a newly acquired one.

In practice, it seems impossible to engage several thousands of customers in an intimate way such as is being described here for an RDHY organisation. However, engaging the customer does not necessarily mean taking a one-to-one approach unless your company wishes to have only a few customers. Additionally, the internal capacity of your organisation may not allow you to have a one-to-one interaction with your customers. Haier Japan recognises this and deploys a customer engagement technique that captures customer insights through collaborative platforms with emerging themes from the bigger data taken on board. Feedback loops are kept open so that at the broader level, customers feel engaged and valued. An emerging theme from the customer engagement process is then actively worked on by both customers and employees and the outcome is one that ensures customer loyalty, which ultimately delivers growth. Bain & Company together with Harvard Business School scholar W. Earl Sasser demonstrated that increasing customer loyalty by 5% has the potential to deliver growth in profits by 25%–95%. This is corroborated by Wharton's *Marketing Metrics*, which puts the probability of selling to a loyal customer at between 60% to 70% in contrast to 5%–25% for a new customer.

What makes customers (users) easily distracted?

The twenty-first century is one that can be described as the age of intelligence and analytics. The key distinguishing factor for this era is the central role of digital data in driving decisions by both users and companies. Technological platforms are vehicles for collecting and transmitting large amounts of data at great speeds and organising this data for strategic decisions. For users, there is a lot of organised data or information being thrown at them on a continuous basis. Companies, for instance, track user activity on their platforms in order to understand user interests over time. When such information is put together meaningfully, it can generate a picture of users, which is then used to send targeted information about products and services that would appeal to the user. Given that e-commerce is well entrenched in many parts of the world, customers who engage in online purchases inadvertently leave digital footprints from multiple site visits and these are captured by many organisations for tailored marketing purposes. By contrast, users of social media platforms voluntarily give out more specific information about themselves and their likes or dislikes, and such information is also harvested by companies. Digital marketing has become a domain which is fast gaining prominence and new career roles are emerging within this space. What all of these imply is that a technology-driven, interconnected world creates conditions that could potentially cause distractions for the customer. Why is it important to pay attention to this? If an organisation invests in customers, it also wants to ensure customer loyalty, as this is what guarantees repeat purchases and a continuous flow of revenue.

The factors leading to a distracted customer can be viewed from two perspectives: factors from within the customer and factors external to the customer. Needs, tastes and preferences are factors internal to the customer and they determine what direction customers go in to find solutions to their needs. However, such needs must not be seen as static, as argued in earlier sections. Additionally, as users move from one generational group to another, or from one life phase to the next, their priorities, needs and values may become less predictable or may change, such that their lifestyle becomes dictated by these new values. These emergent changes represent potential instability which then moves customers into conditions where they can be easily influenced by other brands offering solutions to their changing needs. As a result, businesses cannot simply assume that customers' demands can be predicted, as they are likely to change their minds based on internal factors, as explained earlier.

Another cause of distraction for a customer is the absence of loyalty to an existing brand.[11] Where a customer is indifferent between brands, it is easy to become distracted by a plethora of offers claiming to provide solutions to the customer's needs. The EMC model aims to address this key problem by involving users in product ideation and product development. As equal stakeholders in the partnership, they become locked into long-term relationships with organisations. Importantly, they are committed to the success of the enterprise because of the benefits accruing to them in the mutually beneficial relationship. While they provide the necessary data on their needs and preferences in addition to ideas for new or modified products, they also benefit from having their needs met and a company dedicated to continuously meeting emerging needs. They help to provide feedback on early prototypes of products, thereby being involved in research and development activities. EMCs in the Internet of Things typify this long-term connection with users which offers a solution to the problem of distraction. It is worth noting, however, that against the backdrop of aggressive advertising activities by competing brands and the presence of alternatives offering similar solutions to customer needs, except if there are specific contractual agreements precluding customers from engaging with multiple companies simultaneously, the customer–organisation relationship is only held together by mutual trust and commitment. This places a huge premium on social values that keep society cohesive and maintain its continued existence. The challenge of this is that social values vary across societies and therefore what acts as a strong form of social control in one social context may not be as effective in another.

Successful strategies for achieving customer loyalty – Haier's Smart Cooking EMC

Through Haier's ecosystem approach, it has been able to expand its product offerings to users by having a deep understanding of user lifestyles and needs. It was able to transition from a home appliance manufacturer to solutions provider for customers. For instance, its main product line was expanded into the food preparation space, where chefs were involved in designing solutions for customers, such that they could now make restaurant-quality meals at home (see Case Study 4.1). The roast duck is one such successful result of meeting the need for this product. However,

> ## Case Study 4.1
>
> ### Haier's Smart Cooking EMC
>
> Ecosystem micro-communities (EMCs) in Haier engage their customers through ecosystems based on the RDHY principle and draw on the power of technology and advanced analytics to create enduring customer relationships. One of Haier's EMCs that emerged is the Haier Smart Home headed by Wu Yong, Vice President of Haier Smart Home and Owner of the Kitchen Appliance Platform, which takes care of customer kitchen connectivity as well as smart home services generally in China. A business opportunity was identified with millennials who wanted a more user-friendly and smarter kitchen. As a result, a Smart Cooking EMC was spun out of the Smart Home EMC in 2019 and headed by Zhang Yu. The intention was to combine smart appliances with the Internet of Food (IoF), which is associated with user diet and nutrition to produce a new solution for the customer. Wu Yong details what sets his business apart from others by stressing how the move towards an ecosystem approach under the RDHY management philosophy was particularly suited for the IoF organisation he runs. This ecosystem considered customers as organisational members and was therefore consistent with the very architecture of what IoF seeks to achieve technologically, that is, to connect relevant entities and people without prejudice. For instance, the kitchen fridge could be easily connected to an expert cook whose recipes are readily accessible by the customer wanting to cook a meal. This IoF business began as a result of changing customer needs in the Chinese market. A growing middle class was no longer only interested in buying home appliances but also wanted the

> opportunity to enjoy meals that were both local and exotic. To do so, Haier's solution of the IoF was apt, as it supplied the appliances as well as the means to make whatever meal the customer wanted.
>
> To grow this IoF business, Yong deployed three main stages as necessary ingredients without which the business could not deliver value to customers. The first stage was one of co-creation of added value. This stage involved working collaboratively with partners and employees to innovate ways by which the average customer could cook meals that otherwise required special expertise, e.g. Chinese roast duck. The second stage was that of added value sharing. This stage involved a strengthening of the network of relations that formed the IoF, including a recruitment of nine chefs, a release of 19% equity in order to attract more ecosystem partners who would have ownership of the business, and a reinvestment of profits into the ecosystem in order to expand customer offerings. The final stage was one of further expansion through venture capital in order to make the ecosystem even more robust. This also involved the recruitment of several hundred chefs and various platform developments for managing IoF services ranging from customer purchasing to customer food cooking and customer food supply.

the company continued to seek ways to deepen its relationship with customers and moved into time-efficient product offerings. Making a quick breakfast was seen as a need in many families and so the EMC created some breakfast scenarios where people could cook a meal while getting washed or dressed for work. Haier also expanded from the prestigious but low-frequency roast duck to more high-frequency, daily meal products. As a result, they had to bring on board several other resource providers. While the main suppliers for the roast duck product would have been limited to duck breeders or meat food manufacturers, for the higher-frequency products, they could now integrate several suppliers into the value chain, such as chefs, pastry stores, appliance manufacturers and food factories. The result was that user experiences improved and the EMC ecosystem became a platform for connecting a wide range of partners.

This IoF enterprise, through its customer connections, works collaboratively to create, capture and deliver value to customers by discussing customer needs and solutions. It considers customer desires for various meals – which other organisations might dismiss as mundane – an important driver of its customer relationship. This approach creates a feeling of belonging for the customer who sees their gustatory desires and aspirations met by the enterprise. In this instance, an interconnection of various partners, employees, customers and the organisation makes the IoF enterprise an open-bordered organisation, with the customer valued as an equal member. These strategies have allowed Haier to continue to offer value to its stakeholders. Importantly, all members have value to offer and operate interdependently based on the principle of equality and autonomy. The technological platform and leadership provided by Haier facilitate the realisation of such multiple value streams, ultimately delivering customer loyalty.[12]

How to engage the distracted customer

Knowing that the average customer makes buying decisions in conditions where multiple brands and product offerings make it easy to become distracted, there is a need for contemporary organisations to have a strategic plan for engaging the customer.[13] Research shows that when a customer is engaged, there is a positive contribution to returns on investments.

The principle of RDHY offers a way for the customer to channel his or her energies into a specific organisation, contributing to the development of products and services that meet customer needs. Having a shared understanding of the values underpinning the relationship, which is based on equality, is foundational to having loyal customers. Communicating this new way of perceiving the customer can be empowering because it offers the customer partnership status in a mutually beneficial relationship with your organisation. Equality is also not just within the enterprise – employees and customers alike – but it extends to the broader ecosystem and wider society, thereby reinforcing the value of the EMC model to society. While the EMC itself is a node within the organisation, every member of the EMC is also a node, with autonomy, dignity and potential waiting to be released. Each EMC (see Figure 4.1) is also focused on showing and bringing their value on board.

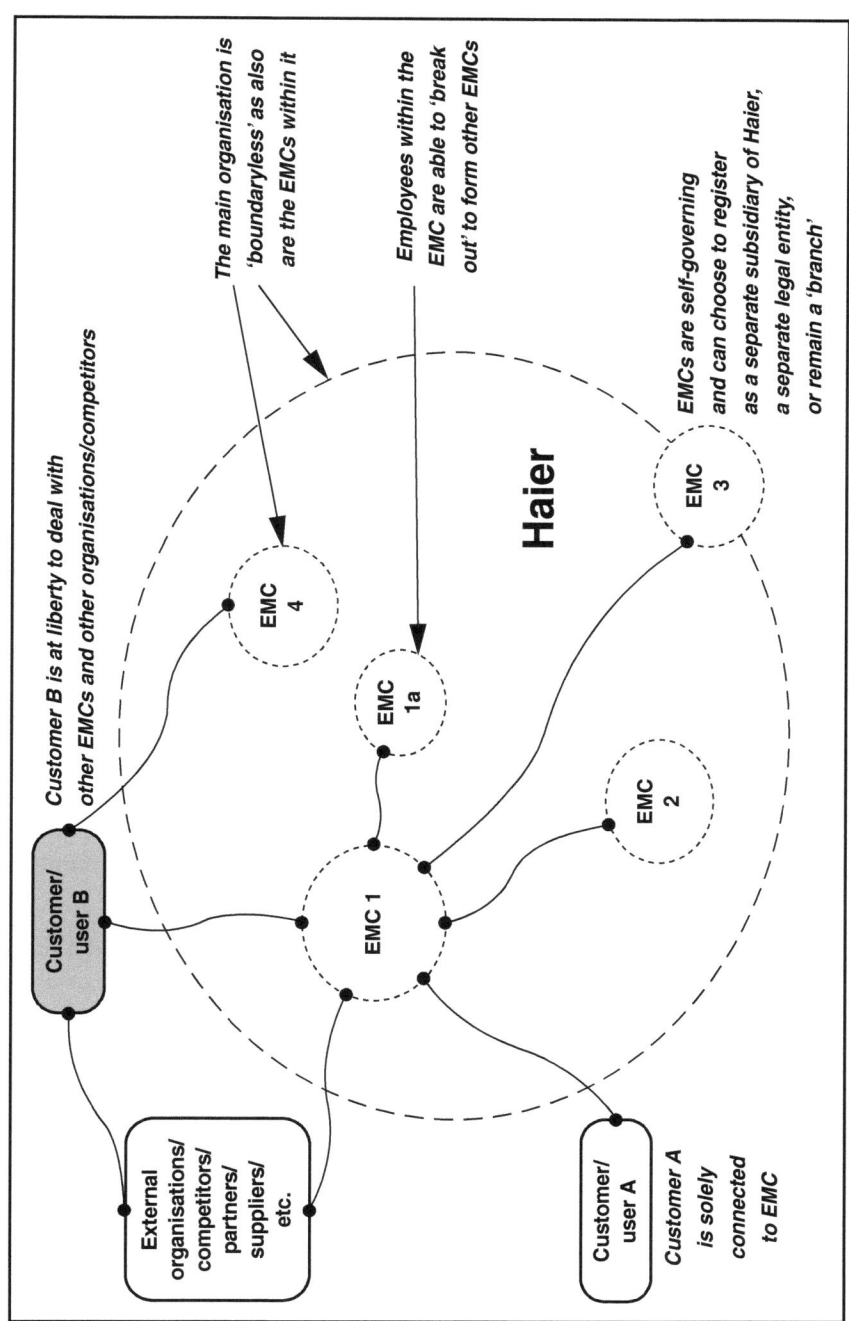

Figure 4.1 The distracted customer in the EMC.

Your key role as a leader in an ecosystem is therefore to create conditions that facilitate the expression of this value and getting your customers to develop a deep connection with your brand. For example, the success and expansion of Haier's Smart Laundry EMC, known as Mr.Hi Smart+, can be attributed to meeting user needs but also to an EMC brand. The EMC recognised that self-laundry was popular amongst users, identified problems with the existing products and leveraged technology to create smart solutions to long washing times. The smart technology in Mr.Hi Smart+ also resolves the problems associated with booking appointments at laundromats in community stores in Thailand. In this way, it created value for users. In a recent publication entitled 'The magic that makes customer experiences stick',[14] Stefan Thomke noted that creating value is key to delivering memorable experiences for the customer. Achieving this requires that your company creates opportunities for customers to make emotional connections with your brand. Articulating the things that are meaningful to customers and positioning yourself in that space provide a way for customers to make links between the two, e.g. running adverts that communicate that the company recognises significant moments in a customer's life, such as the birth of children, educational attainments, weddings, and purchase of property or other personal assets. These are moments that elicit an emotional response in customers and, over time, repeated advertisements or promotions on these become associated with the company's brand in the minds of customers. This is an effective way to keep the customer mindful of your brand.

You can utilise the analytic tools provided by social media platforms that generate customer activity, such as short surveys, comments, online reviews giving feedback on new products, crowdsourcing product ideas or customer competitions with prizes for winners. Vice President at Tata Consultancy Services, Sudhakar Gudala, along with management scholars John Hauser and Artem Timoshenko,[13] showed that active customer engagement contributes to enhanced experiences and satisfaction but also to increased revenues for companies. You can also engage the distracted customer by leveraging technology and data analytics to produce meaningful responses to customer needs, as a recent study by Ross et al., 'Creating digital offerings that customers will buy', suggests.[15] To illustrate, Haier Germany was able to navigate the challenges of the lockdown period caused by the COVID-19 pandemic. Through its proactive engagement with data, it developed a strategy to continue to maintain supply lines for its channel customers while other local German suppliers shut down their factories as they had no back-up measures in place. Additionally, a company's sense-making of data mined from customers' digital footprints can explore multiple dimensions of the customer such as age, gender, lifestyle, including health factors, nutrition and exercise, as well as influences on the customer from the media and technology trends. This learning can then be deployed as add-on benefits to existing products.[16] While data analytics offers benefits, there are also downsides that need to be addressed for customer engagement to work successfully. Increasingly, customers express concerns with confidentiality, data protection and issues of cybersecurity. It is important to anticipate and respond to these concerns. In summary, the key points regarding how to engage the distracted customer include:

- Leveraging technology to proactively anticipate shifting trends and making suggestions for new solutions.
- Helping the customer to connect emotionally with your brand and involving the customer in co-creating solutions.
- Creating solutions that respond to customer needs and speak to customer aspirations.
- Deepening customer commitment and ownership by offering a stake in the business via rewards, remuneration and partnership.

Chapter summary, reflective questions and practical implications

Your orientation about the customer is fundamental to how your business engages with the customer. It determines your decisions around organisational policies, your rationalisation for expenditure on services that impact on customer experience, how you segment and select the markets to serve and the development of products and solutions for those markets. There is a need to rethink your conventional perceptions of the customer, given the closer connectivity across markets and technology platforms.

Globalisation and developments in information and communication technologies have resulted in integrated markets, greater collaboration and strategic alliances which produce ecosystems. The implication of these conditions is that customers are faced with more choices than ever before and, as a result, wield greater power in the marketplace. Indeed, it has become a buyer's market. For your business to operate in a sustainable way, therefore, there needs to be a shift in your thinking regarding the role of the customer – no longer as a replaceable external party to the organisation but as fundamental to its continued existence. While the dichotomy between customers and organisations may have been a long-held tradition, focusing on what value the customer can add enables you to give them increasing attention. The RDHY model of engaging the customer expresses this shift from traditional conceptions of the customer–organisation connection to that of ecosystems. Across many of its companies, Haier represents this new philosophy and offers platforms that support the continued symbiotic relationship with users. The growing success of the Internet of Things and the expansion of EMC ecosystems suggest that a deep knowledge of the customer in this new orientation offers some positive results.

The rise of consumerism has contributed to greater awareness of the need for businesses to be accountable along several dimensions, including how they demonstrate responsiveness to users as part of their key stakeholders. As a result, your customer has taken centre stage in the world of business, and increasingly there is a shift away from the basic expectation that the purpose of the customer is solely to provide income to your organisation. This approach to redefining the customer–organisation relationship is therefore a call to closely interrogate your philosophy as a business leader and the values you hold regarding your relationship with your customers or end-users.

In this light, we put forward some reflective questions to prompt a re-evaluation of your orientations about the customer–organisation connection in your organisation.

- *Do you see the customer as fundamentally external to your organisation or internal?* Taking the perspective of customers as integral parts of the organisation allows you to see the potential inherent in a more collaborative approach to running your business with the customer intrinsically involved. You need to demonstrate the courage to devolve some 'power' to your customers. This can be done by encouraging customers to participate in decision-making within the organisation and letting them know how and when their input has produced results. A link that opens up an area for customer voice on your website could be a starting point. Be open and transparent, as these are values that signal to your customer that their interests are taken seriously, and they can trust your new partnership with them to deliver on its promise. Indeed, the trust is a reciprocal one.

- *How well do you involve the customer in your processes as regards new product development?* Involving the customer in new product development allows you to demonstrate a level of trust in the customer. By deploying resources to product development, you are able to show that you trust the information coming from the customer and are willing to feed these into strategic decision-making. From brainstorming on ideas to modifications on prototypes and finished products, your customer represents current and future demand and therefore should be at the heart of your decision-making. (As an example, see Case Study 5.2 on FirstBuild as they use their CoCreate platform to engage with customers for product innovation.)

- *Do you understand the profile of your current customers?* One of the key ways to retain customers is to have a deep knowledge of customer profiles. Here, a cursory approach is of little value in a globally competitive world. There is a need to understand your customers deeply and explore the opportunities for learning about them through ongoing conversations and analysis of their social or buying habits. Using technology, you can mine the data you have on your customers to understand them by age, gender, occupation or buying patterns. This technological approach can sometimes be considered as being overly intrusive to customer habits and online footprints. We throw in a bit of caution here as it is important that you appropriately seek customer consent.

- *What do you know of your customers' aspirations?* Beyond understanding the profiles of existing customers, it is important to realise that, as with many things, needs, tastes, interests and preferences change over time, and as a business you need to understand the drivers of these changes and keep tracking the changes. It is important to deepen your engagement, relationship and communication with your customers to uncover these aspirations. By encouraging your customers to engage with your social media platforms and share their thoughts on the performance of current products and ideas for desirable solutions or by analysing their browsing habits, you will be able to gauge not just their profiles but also their aspirations. Sometimes a direct engagement through customer research can help.

- *Can you identify any patterns or shifts in your customer tastes and preferences across different demographics?* With the availability of various survey instruments online, you can run market surveys or validation experiments across different demographics to gain insight into your market space. Although there may be individual differences in user preferences, it is beneficial also to have a system for identifying broad patterns emerging from the data generated across different demographics. For instance, understanding changing lifestyle practices can be studied across the working population (labour force) or the ageing population. Analysing structural and temporal trends offers opportunities for new product development, which may become solutions to needs users may not yet be aware of. As one group of users transitions into another, the common denominator is an organisation that is nimble, proactive and responsive.

References

1. Rodriguez, B. (2018) 'Putting customer experience at the center of digital transformation', *MIT Sloan Management Review*, available at https://sloanreview.mit.edu/article/putting-customer-experience-at-the-center-of-digital-transformation/(accessed 15 November 2022).
2. Westerman, G. (2017) 'Your company doesn't need a digital strategy', *MIT Sloan Management Review*, available at https://sloanreview.mit.edu/article/your-company-doesnt-need-a-digital-strategy/ (accessed 15 November 2022).
3. Hotten, R. (2020) 'Elon Musk tweet wipes $14bn off Tesla's value', *BBC News*, available at https://www.bbc.co.uk/news/business-52504187 (accessed 15 November 2022).

4. Meyer, D. (2021) 'Tesla has lost more than $200 billion in market value since Elon Musk's Twitter poll—costing him 15% of his fortune so far', *Fortune*, available at https://fortune.com/2021/11/10/tesla-stock-slide-elon-musk-twitter-poll-tsla/ (accessed 15 November 2022).
5. Rost, J. (1995) 'Leadership: a discussion about ethics', *Business Ethics Quarterly*, 5(1): 129–142.
6. Training Magazine (2019) *2109 Training Industry Report*, available at https://trainingmag.com/sites/default/files/2019_industry_report.pdf (accessed 15 November 2022).
7. Pontefract, D. (2019) 'The Wasted Dollars Of Corporate Training Programs', *Forbes*, available at https://www.forbes.com/sites/danpontefract/2019/09/15/the-wasted-dollars-of-corporate-training-programs/?sh=5896c36b71f9 (accessed 15 November 2022).
8. Oberlo (n.d.) 'Mobile commerce sales in 2022', available at https://www.oberlo.co.uk/statistics/mobile-commerce-sales (accessed 15 November 2022).
9. Stansell, A. (2019) 'Entering the job market? Here are the highest paying entry level jobs and internships for 2019', Glassdoor Economic Research, available at https://www.glassdoor.com/research/internships-entry-level-jobs-2019/ (accessed 15 November 2022).
10. IDC (2021) 'Global spending on big data and analytics solutions will reach $215.7 billion in 2021, according to a new IDC spending guide', IDC Solutions, available at https://www.idc.com/getdoc.jsp?containerId=prUS48165721 (accessed 15 November 2022).
11. Grand View Research, *Customer experience management market size, share & trends analysis report by analytical tools, by touch point type, by deployment, by end-use, by region, and segment forecasts, 2022–2030*, available at https://www.grandviewresearch.com/industry-analysis/customer-experience-management-market (accessed 15 November 2022).
12. Farris, P. W., Bendle, N., Pfeifer, P. & Reibstein, D. (2011) *Marketing metrics: the definitive guide to measuring marketing performance*, 2nd edition. Wharton School series. Pearson.

13. Gudala, S., Hauser, J. R. & Timoshenko, A. (2019) 'The new era of personalization: why CPG brands must own the direct-to-consumer experience', *MIT Sloan Management Review*, available at https://sloanreview.mit.edu/sponsors-content/the-new-era-of-personalization-why-cpg-brands-must-own-the-direct-to-consumer-experience/ (accessed 15 November 2022).

14. Thomke, S. (2019) 'The magic that makes customer experiences stick', *MIT Sloan Management Review*, available at https://sloanreview.mit.edu/article/the-magic-that-makes-customer-experiences-stick/ (accessed 15 November 2022).

15. Ross, J. W., Beath, C. M. & Mocker, M. (2019) 'Creating digital offerings that customers will buy', *MIT Sloan Management Review*, available at https://sloanreview.mit.edu/article/creating-digital-offerings-customers-will-buy/ (accessed 15 November 2022).

16. Wixom, B. H., Schüritz, R. M. & Farrell. K. (2020) 'Why smart companies are giving customers more data', *MIT Sloan Management Review*, available at https://sloanreview.mit.edu/article/why-smart-companies-are-giving-customers-more-data/ (accessed 15 November 2022).

Chapter 5

The corporate need is simple – its employees

Introduction

This chapter considers the relationship between employees and the organisation. We begin by describing the employee according to RenDanHeYi (RDHY): employees are highly sought-after powerhouses of capabilities that organisations need to meet the needs of the customer. They are also 'freer' than ever – the notion of 'the company man' is finished in the fourth industrial revolution and a highly competitive talent marketplace. With case studies, we consider the need for investment in employee engagement and company culture, and explain how to implement and reinforce the RDHY culture for new and existing employees. Factors to be discussed include culture and shared cognition, process, people factors and creating a psychologically safe climate for employees to engage in activities that help to improve connections between employees and customers. Top tips prompt readers from every level and function on how to start engaging the two groups immediately.

Employees as powerhouses of capabilities

Employees constitute one of the key aspects of organisations in the sense that they are often seen as part of the array of resources available to a firm in its productive activities. In contrast to resources such as land, capital, buildings or stock, humans are valued because of the labour they provide. This labour can be understood from two perspectives: that of 'brawn' and 'brain'. While 'brawn' refers to physical capabilities which are used for manual dimensions of work, 'brain' refers to higher cognitive capabilities that are deployed in pooling together all other resources in the organisation, in strategic thinking and in creative and analytical activities.

As a result, employees are a unique type of organisational resource because of the ability to organise other resources for productive use, but also the ability to engage in creative work. While human beings can be broadly categorised in this way, there are unique differences between people which afford them the opportunity to showcase capabilities that are difficult to copy or imitate both within and outside the organisation. This unique combination of aptitudes, abilities and skill sets allows employees to function as powerhouses of capabilities which are relevant where the customer is concerned. As humans, employees are able to understand customers from an empathetic standpoint and thus apply their skills in understanding their needs but also in creating solutions to those needs. As opposed to interacting with artificial intelligence, customers are able to communicate meaningfully with employees and similarly receive meaningful feedback. The human has a capacity for continuous learning and therefore one can expect that as employees continuously integrate new learning with existing experience, new solutions can be created to meet emerging challenges. What is important to note is that at the centre of this dynamic knowledge terrain are the customer's current and future needs.

Why are employees highly sought-after when it comes to meeting the needs of customers? Leaders in organisations recognise the value that employees bring to the workplace in terms of contributing to productivity, innovation and creativity. Employees implement the strategies designed by leaders in relation to increasing market share, growth, product innovation and processes that support organisational activities. Beyond these, however, employees are able to analyse current trends in customer practices, understand customer priorities and project what implications these may have for future needs across industries. This information is invaluable for an organisation that wants to retain loyal customers and sustain its market share. Having a holistic and ongoing understanding of the customer is necessary for remaining relevant in meeting the customer's needs. Within an RDHY framework, understanding the customer becomes even more critical, as the competitive landscape potentially presents opportunities and threats. There are opportunities to create new product lines, develop new markets and grow with the customer. However, there are also threats from competing firms which are also constantly scanning the landscape and presenting alternatives to customers, which may cause them to switch between firms. Despite the benefits of artificial intelligence, human resources offer inimitable capabilities which give competitive advantage to firms.

Employee mobility and the talent marketplace

Working patterns of employees have traditionally reflected loyalty to organisations, which often leads to staying with a single organisation for the majority of their working years until retirement. This type of work pattern is one where employees rise through the ranks over years of working in the same role or across different roles. Employers have also found value in offering lifetime employment to workers as a way to manage employee turnover, as shown in Ouchi's Theory Z, where successful performance of Japanese businesses in the 1970s was attributed to an employee-centred corporate culture, which encouraged employee ownership of company shares, lifetime employment and promotion based on seniority. But contemporary organisations have experienced a dynamic shift from such patterns, whereby employees no longer aim to work for a lifetime in a single organisation but move across several organisations.

Many factors account for this dynamism in the labour market and the market for talent. They include internal and external labour market changes. In an internal labour market change, employees come into or leave organisations as a result of the introduction of several factors, such as new technology, changes to organisational structure such as mergers and acquisitions, staff going away on maternity or paternity leave and the introduction of incoming staff cover for them and specialist talent recruitment. External labour market changes, on the other hand, could be related to increases in the supply of available talent or qualified professionals for a role, changes in market demands which require upskilling and new hiring, technological advancements across industries, factors which affect the pricing of labour and an increase in the competitive landscape, whereby more organisations come into sectors as a result of low entry barriers or competitive advantage in relation to cost or nearness to raw materials or resources. These changes create a need for the movement of employees from one organisation to another. In some cases, employees leave paid employment to set up their own businesses and, by doing so, add to the number of players within the competitive space or industry. At other times, employees move from one employer to another.

There are also employer pull factors (see Figure 5.1) that contribute to the mobility of talent in the marketplace. Employers often compete to offer attractive remuneration packages in exchange for their fresh talent or expertise. Inadvertently, this competition for talent creates a buyers' market, where employees have a stronger bargaining power and may contribute to determining higher pricing for talent. While the relative value of talent can be associated with what employers are willing to pay to attract and retain employees, it is worth noting that due to advances in technology and other wider socioeconomic factors affecting the demand for talent, we can expect knowledge to become outdated over time, which then requires upskilling of existing employees or engagement of new ones. The talent marketplace is indeed a dynamic one where several actors contribute to determining the supply, demand,

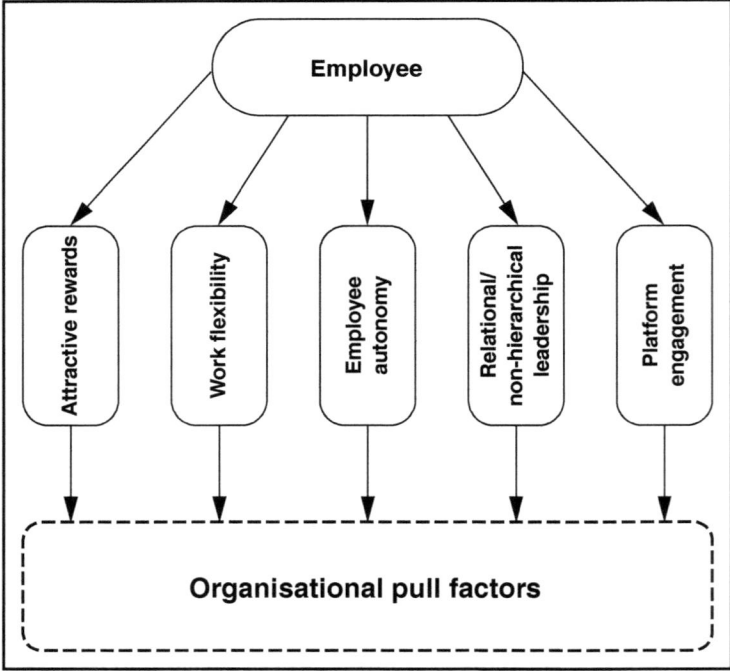

Figure 5.1 Organisational pull factors keeping employees.

pricing and development of human resources. What enables an organisation to reap returns on investment in its human resources is the ability to retain such talent and enjoy capabilities that are unique and often difficult to imitate, contributing to a company's competitive advantage. A notable factor in retaining key talent is how well an organisation is able to keep employees engaged.

The need for investment in employee engagement

Employee engagement is a nebulous concept and, as a result, it is often not clear how to do it. Without knowing the 'what' of employee engagement, the activities or processes that must be deployed to engage employees become elusive. Management scholar William Kahn offered an initial definition of the concept of engagement in his seminal work 'Psychological conditions of personal engagement and disengagement at work' as 'the harnessing of organisation members' selves to their work roles; in engagement, people employ and express themselves physically, cognitively, and emotionally during role performances'. This original perspective on employee engagement means the organisation risks losing employees to presenteeism, i.e. they may be at work but are not really connected to their tasks, be it physically, cognitively or emotionally. Organisations must therefore seek to invest in employee engagement if they wish to succeed in the competitive space. To engage employees, management scholar Ray Baumruk argues it requires a 'fire in the belly', i.e. employees need to be passionate at an emotional level about their work.

The implication is that employee engagement is not a one-off activity. It is not a day's workshop with a consultant as the star of the day, nor is it a company policy carefully written out but often with managerial mumbo jumbo. Employee engagement is a cognitive state that is directly reflected in embodied actions that are visible enough to be contagious within an organisation. It is not imparted via a unidirectional speech from the CEO, nor is it whipped up among employees by some motivational talk. Employee engagement happens when it is intrinsically connected to employees' sense of self. It is generated from personhood and the *raison d'être* of employees' work. It comes from the *why* of work.

To invest in employee engagement is to address conditions in the work environment that allow the personhood of the employee to flourish. In our words, employee engagement is a human-centric concept which must not be reduced to workshops or training sessions and so on. The organisation's task is to build a climate that allows engagement to happen. If there is any external push factor, it has to be the willingness of the organisation to be radical, to swim against the tide of orthodoxy and to simply do things differently.

Employee engagement is therefore about the organisational climate generated that allows individuals to realise their true potentials. The 'self' must be liberated within the organisation to let the individuality of employees flourish at work. William Khan, whose seminal work kickstarted the stream of research on employee engagement, was careful to note that employee engagement occurs at the level of employee self-hood. If employee engagement is not first at the level of personal engagement, the organisation is unlikely to yield its benefits. At the level of the self, employees must be at liberty to start something on their own (see Case Study 5.1).

Case Study 5.1

Creating Gmail

Paul Buchheit, an employee of Google, offers us a prime example of the idea of employee self-expression. Buchheit had a dream of building a web-based email long before joining Google as its 23rd employee in 1999. However, Google's policy allowing 20% of employee work hours for experimentation created a conducive environment for the success of Buchheit's dream. Google launched its Gmail on 1 April 2004 and the rest is history. Not only did he take the task as accomplishing something for himself, he also added to Google's portfolio of products, and in the process Gmail's own suite of other applications would emerge. Prior to Gmail, Google's main business focus was on online search. Today, Google is known for more than just being a search engine.

We find that RDHY offers the possibility to make this happen, only this time employees are able to devote 100% of their time to pursuing the building of a new ecosystem micro-community (EMC). Being a management philosophy, RDHY carries a DNA that runs through an organisation's culture so that employees are not told to engage, but they simply engage because 'that is the way things are around here'. In other words, the self can express itself and employ itself in a culture that is the seedbed for engagement.

The need for investment in company culture

Culture in an organisation can often be difficult to grasp, due to its multifaceted nature. It is a term that encompasses beliefs, symbols, values, norms, myths, rituals and practices. A lot of the time, culture is simplistically equated with practices and, because of this perspective, there is an assumption that it can be created, changed and adjusted by the manager. This perspective again tacitly assumes that the key actors – managers – are themselves distinct from the culture, hence their positioning as external agents who bring about cultural change through organisational action. In reality, organisational culture involves all members of an organisation.

Far from a mainstream view which sees culture as defined solely by organisational leaders, culture reflects what is valued in an organisation and that, in turn, is expressed in many other aspects of organisational life. This view considers all voices in an organisation and, from this standpoint, organisations reflect meeting points of different value systems, from direct owners, managers and workers to other external stakeholders. These values drive decision-making and strategic actions and, in turn, influence the performance of companies. Culture begins to crystallise where there is a shared system of meaning; however, the achievement of this shared cognition cannot be left to chance. There is a need for companies to be deliberate about investing in culture and shared cognition. Central points of reference are powerful rallying points for organisational members, as they help to align company goals with individual actions. Shared knowledge, shared narratives, shared history and shared values produce strong cultures where organisational members understand the company vision and how to get there. This makes the job of a leader easier as, in the words of leadership scholar Gary Yukl, people would 'understand and agree about what needs to be done and how to do it'. Companies need to invest in understanding their employees and providing what they need to succeed in their roles. Additionally, there is a need to initiate activities that foster a sense of shared purpose and build communities of workers who understand the overall vision of the organisation and how their individual work fits into achieving it. Such initiatives include formal and informal sessions where the organisational values are shared with employees, but, more importantly, sessions where these values are demonstrated – for instance, celebrating and recognising employee achievements, creating opportunities for employee participation and a voice in company strategic plans, and providing opportunities to support employee growth and development.

Company culture can also be seen in organisational processes such as recruitment or processes guiding promotions and career advancement. Such processes should reflect values of inclusion, diversity and equity, which enable the company to attract and retain employees that can strengthen its competitive advantage. Many companies espouse people as their most important assets and, as such, there is a need for an organisation to 'walk the talk' and invest in hiring, retaining and developing its people. This approach to investing in employees contributes to a culture that facilitates creativity and innovation, and in which organisational members can thrive. It creates a psychologically safe climate for employees to engage in activities that can improve the needed connections between employees and customers, which is at the core of the RDHY philosophy.

Implementing and reinforcing the RDHY culture for new and existing employees

The philosophy of RDHY is incomplete without a culture that sustains it. To implement RDHY within an organisation, we need to think of a practical framework that allows employees to flourish within the tenets that RDHY espouses.

An appreciation of the ecosystem era at the heart of RDHY offers us the opportunity to experiment with actionable ideas within the organisation (as detailed in Chapter 1). This is because an ecosystem imposes pull and push effects on a varied number of interconnected actors, holding all members together. The implication is that actionable steps are constantly taken in order to ensure the success of the ecosystem. Take Haier entrepreneur Liu Zhanjie as an example. Attracted to Haier's entrepreneurship programme, Liu Zhanjie left his job as a university lecturer and joined Haier's research and development department in 2001. In 2005, as RDHY slowly became embedded as the DNA of the organisation, Liu Zhanjie made an ambitious but successful bid to lead the biomedical unit of the business, thus becoming its owner. Having managed to raise a team of other employees, they soon set off to identify user needs as well as opportunities like Internet of Things (IoT) that could help to meet user needs. Zhanjie and his team soon grew to 30 employees who committed themselves to a mission of building their own EMC and together delivered outstanding results year-on-year. In October 2019, Haier Biomedical underwent a successful initial public offering (IPO). Through this framework of the EMC, Liu Zhanjie thus transformed from being an employee to becoming the CEO of a public company. Haier Biomedical's market capitalisation has since increased from approximately $1.4 billion at IPO to over $6 billion. Its staff size also grew from the initial 30 to more than 2,000 employees, 67 of whom received stock incentives.

The RDHY culture that is sustained through EMCs ensures that its human-centric philosophy permeates through the organisation as employees express themselves, take ownership and deliver value both for themselves and for their customers. Haier calls this a 'maximisation of human value', manifesting in a kind of cycle (from reinventing value → delivering value → sharing value), thus allowing the value created to be captured by both users and employees. It is in this sense a case of creating an atmosphere that allows *intra*preneurs to emerge, supporting those *intra*preneurial minds to eventually create their own operational ecosystems. This inside-out approach departs from acquisition models often observed in organisations in the West where cultural integration issues plague various mergers and acquisitions.

Another example of the idea of employees delivering value for the customer is seen in Haier's Internet of Food (IoF) EMC (as illustrated in Chapter 4). The mantra here is: 'What users need is not just a great kitchen, but great food.' The IoF EMC's insights into users' real needs led them to form partnerships with other actors to create an ecosystem that allows users to access dish menus from the comfort of their own kitchens. Initially through connection to smart ovens and refrigerators, users are able to access menus like 'one-click roast duck' for a home dining experience. After more than 100 iterations, IoF founder Zhang Yu and roast duck chef Zhang Weili now provide users with various one-click menus. IoF has since sold more than 300,000 roast ducks through Haier ovens, becoming the third largest roast duck restaurant in China without the traditional brick-and-mortar presence.

The deployment of RDHY management models through its EMCs thus breaks the boundaries of traditional enterprises and maximises value for all actors within the ecosystem. In practice, an EMC is organised through a formal contract with employees, thus bringing structure to organised chaos.

The EMC contract: price war example

The basis of the EMC contract and its effectiveness lie in the fact that it is founded on the value of equilibrium. Through the EMC contract, EMCs achieve the Nash equilibrium of a combination of strategies. In other words, those who operate within this framework are clear that what they do and how they engage is optimal for all.

Consider what happens in the all-too-familiar world of price wars. A company decides to retain customers and attracts consumers by offering the lowest possible price. It may be lucrative in the short term but often fails to create sustainable value as other players with perhaps bigger wallets can offset any gains made in the price war. If, however, companies pursue a strategy that seeks to avoid a price war in the interests of all, each party would then seek to align around an optimal strategic outcome for all involved. This requires discipline and a belief in the creation of a value cycle. The fragility lies in the possibility of the equilibrium breaking when and if a single act is taken that negates the agreed approach. This is not to say that competitors come together to agree on their own individual outcomes; instead, by their unique strategies, an 'invisible' equilibrium may be sustained or broken. In the case of the latter, businesses are left in a position that no longer represents the optimal strategy.

For Haier's EMC contracts, the Nash equilibrium achieved, as measured by an 'RDHY scorecard', ensures a positive outcome in that all players involved work towards creating a shared value in contrast to the highly individualistic thinking in various other markets and business organisations. In an EMC, created value becomes shared value and this is reflected in the monetary awards for all employees. For instance, in double-entry bookkeeping, invented in Italy in the fifteenth century and commonly used worldwide, the principle is that 'every debit always has a corresponding credit, and the total debits and total credits are always equal'. For instance, on the balance sheet, a piece of equipment may be marked with a value of $1 million on the asset side. Correspondingly, we must also see this $1 million either as a liability or potentially as owner's equity and so on. Perhaps it may show as a purchase made or a loan received, etc. Ultimately, both sides of the balance sheet must be reconciled to the last cent. This straightforward thinking in the balance sheet is not what is often observed in the unpredictable world of business where value created and shared is often not equal or as linear as the analogy of the balance sheet. A designer's design may become a mega-hit, yet the designer may only receive the value associated with the design when it was first created, i.e. the design fee. This is fair play, or so it seems. After all, the mega-hit signals a bumper payout for the company and its funders in the future. In RDHY, a radical approach is taken to such a scenario. The value-added return is considered a shared value and everyone within the EMC shares in the product's market mega-hit. The human-centric underpinning of RDHY's EMCs means that individuals are highly motivated and self-led with no singular point of authority dictating progress within the EMC.

The value of the EMC: rooted in balance, growth and co-creation

Haier's EMC contracts are unapologetically rooted in Chinese culture, and its human-centric management philosophy boasts of unparalleled success witnessed in the transformation of failing businesses into global success stories. A closer look reveals some influences in Confucianist and Taoist philosophy also found in influential Chinese cultural material – *The I Ching* or simply the *Book of Changes* – which covers over 3,000 years of cultural influence. According to the *Book of Changes*, one can achieve balance through an understanding of relationalities among various elements. Five elements are mentioned: metal, wood, water, fire and earth. Elements that are near each other in relation to others generate or sustain each other, while those elements further apart tend to restrict each other. In this Taoist thinking as an example, the list in the order as water, wood and fire are relationally adjacent to each other; by their relational positioning, water is nearer to wood and therefore water generates or sustains wood. Equally, wood generates or sustains fire and so on. However, as per the order of the listing, water and fire are relationally distant and therefore water restricts fire, and so on. Similarly, the worldview associated with this Confucian tenet is that a company rises to the top because competitors and co-creators are relationally adjacent, generating, sustaining or restricting one another depending on their relational positioning in the market. As a result, a company must not take its market leadership for granted as it is merely a part of an ecosystem, and the relational alignments may change. This calls for humility, a fundamental human virtue at the core of management.

Danah Zohar's concept of quantum management argues that 'there are no causes, only relationships'. In other words, relationships speak to quantum holism, with the idea that all things are connected. This is seen in the analogy of a manufacturing company that can fail on two counts: inventories and receivables (e.g. high inventories that the company can't sell and vast amounts of receivables that can't be recovered). It becomes a challenge to ascertain the source of the inventory/receivables problems when various departments within the company refuse responsibility for these. This is often the case due to siloed practices, although the company is fundamentally interconnected. For instance, R&D might argue that the design of the product was excellent and therefore the problem must be the manufacturing process. The plant managers might argue that the product was well made and therefore should not be blamed for poor sales. Sales might put the blame on late shipments and logistical support. It becomes a vicious cycle, but also underscoring the connectedness within the company.

In an EMC contract, the connectedness of the ecosystem is taken to a new height, in that it binds everyone together and considers the organisation as one. This way, everyone is responsible for both positive and negative outcomes. As a result, collaborative efforts are interwoven into the fabric of the organisation with employees working towards a common goal. In this way, emergent challenges are collectively dealt with. The EMC contract is therefore open to unforeseen eventualities and is accepted by the organisation. Nobel laureate Oliver Hart posits the idea of incomplete contracts, which assumes that any contract at the time of signing could not exhaustively account for all factors pertinent to the signing parties. Having observed Haier's EMC, Bent Holmstrom, also a Nobel laureate and a co-proponent of the theory of incomplete contracts, reckons that it offers a peek into the future of management especially with IoT at the core. The acknowledgement that the EMC contract could also lead to a complete disaster as challenges emerge along the way allows it to achieve the balance between employees' subjective initiatives and market objectivity.

Operationally, the EMC contract is a co-created phenomenon as employees work together with users to ensure that the objectives of the ecosystem are not jeopardised. The implication is that there is no longer a buyer–seller relationship where the seller creates, captures and delivers value to the customer as we see in traditional business models. It is now a relationship of value co-creation in which there is no prisoner's dilemma. The EMC contract is therefore infinite, continues to self-emerge, self-split, and self-evolve as user experience (re)iterates. At the same time, the EMC contract remains true to what a business ecosystem is meant to be. James F. Moore, who pioneered the business ecosystem theory in 1993, avers that 'co-evolution is a process in which interdependent species evolve in an endless reciprocal cycle'. There is no end to co-creating user experiences, with infinite interactions leading to endless evolution. This is akin to James Carse's words in his 1987 book *Finite and Infinite Games*: 'a finite game is played to win, and an infinite game is played for continuing the play'.

The idea of the EMC contract as an ecosystem contract means that the EMC is not closed but rather a boundaryless self-organisation. In traditional contracts, goals would often be set in relation to internal resources and capabilities. By contrast, the EMC leaves room for active co-creators who are beyond the organisation's employees to be connected to the overall objective (see Case Study 5.2). As of 2022, Haier boasts of more than 4,000 microenterprises and 370 EMCs, forming a networked, non-linear organisational structure. Any identified gaps that emerge are filled as the boundaryless self-organisation ensures its own collective governance, co-creation and sharing across the ecosystem.

Case Study 5.2

FirstBuild's co-creation approach to design

FirstBuild, an innovation laboratory that works with GE Appliances, takes a unique approach in its innovation of new home products or appliances. Instead of a working team of designers who imagine products and build them with the customer in mind, as is the case with traditional design organisations, FirstBuild's approach is one of co-creation. The company harnesses the power of the community to create products that consumers want. This involves employees and consumers working together collaboratively. By engaging the consumer directly, employees at FirstBuild bring innovation to the common marketplace. The company's CoCreate platform allows consumers to engage with employees regarding the design of a product. Anyone can submit ideas and collaborate with FirstBuild employees for home appliances. This has helped to bring innovation to scale for GEA with products that have consumer demands already built in. Taking account of users' own needs, FirstBuild is able to work from conceptualisation of the product through to prototype and then on to the final manufacturing stage. This highly iterative process is done alongside the user at each stage of the design so that a product that is created is actually a co-created product that meets with customer satisfaction as well as employee satisfaction.

Within the company, FirstBuild maintains a policy that encourages employees in participatory innovation projects. Employees are

> involved in each stage of engagement with the customer so that no one is left behind in understanding what objectives are to be met. This has fostered a culture of innovation that considers all ideas equally, allowing what may seem initially to be a non-starter to become a much-desired product. One such example is Mella, a smart edible mushroom-growing home appliance that was brought to life through co-creation with users, mushroom experts, a food expert from Bon Appetit and founders of other mushroom products. As stated on the product's website, 'Mella controls and automates the inputs necessary to grow delicious, edible mushrooms in the comfort of your home.' Whereas the idea of growing mushrooms in one's kitchen may seem odd, engaged employees working in a culture of innovation at FirstBuild leave room for the opportunity to generate something new with consumers who require any home appliance. Mella went on to raise over $550,000 in crowdfunding.
>
> FirstBuild shows how engaged employees willingly take on new challenges to innovate. Employees are able to develop concepts into tangible products and challenge conventional ways of doing work. The culture within the organisation enables this approach to work. It offers a sense of flexibility in how employees do their jobs, encourages networking, stimulates user engagement, leaves room for failure through (re)prototyping, allows self-expression without any inhibitions and is participatory in its characteristic.

Chapter summary, reflective questions and practical implications

Having understood the vital importance of engaged employees, we offer you some ideas for keeping them engaged. Irrespective of your level and function in your organisation, there is something you can do to deepen the connections with your employees. As we have shown in earlier chapters, there is untapped potential waiting to be discovered when employees are given the freedom to become partners with the organisation in mutually beneficial ways. Some reflective questions and practical steps to take into consideration are as follows:

- *Do you really know your employees?* What are their aspirations? You have various data (e.g. date of birth, address, previous employment, education, etc.) about your employees but may often miss the most important data you need for employee engagement. If you know the innermost thoughts of your employees, you will take steps to create an environment where they can thrive. A sense check through conversations and focus groups can go a long way in creating the right organisational climate.

- *How can you leverage the benefits of flexible working for your organisation?* It is almost a cliché to say the world of work is now hybrid. Offer opportunities for your employees to choose how they wish to work. Relinquishing control of the working day to employees signals trust in them. They know work must be done and will use their autonomy to get it done. They will not take a mile when you give them an inch. So, allow your employees to self-determine their working patterns. In this way, you can develop an atmosphere of trust and a great organisational culture.

- *How are you utilising technology?* You can build or use available technology platforms to create avenues for conversations between your employees and customers. For instance, bring your customers into the company by removing boundaries that create ingroups and outgroups. Platforms like FirstBuild's CoCreate can go a long way to help you develop lasting customer–employee networks. At low cost, you can also use your social media channels and online groups for meaningful engagements with your customers. Do not tweet 'at' your customers, tweet 'with' them.

- *What does your organisation's structure look like?* Pursue an EMC approach to building your organisation. The human is at the centre of RDHY, and the need to be one's own boss is an attractive one. The EMC contract is one proven way by which this can be achieved while developing your employees at the same time. Within an EMC, employee–customer engagement is woven into the very fabric of the ecosystem. It takes some reorientation on your part and radical steps, but it makes a huge difference.

Bibliography

Carse, J. P. (2013) *Finite and infinite games: a vision of life as play and possibility*, 1st edition. Free Press.

Derksen, M. (2014) 'Turning men into machines? Scientific management, industrial psychology, and the "human factor"', *Journal of the History of the Behavioral Sciences*. DOI: 10.1002/jhbs.21650

FirstBuild: https://firstbuild.com/

I Ching or Book of Changes: Ancient Chinese wisdom to inspire and enlighten, translated by Wilhelm, R. & Baynes, C. F. (1989). Arkana/Penguin.

Hart, O., & Moore, J. (1988) 'Incomplete contracts and renegotiation', *Econometrica*, 56(4): 755–785.

Khan, W.A. (1990) 'Psychological conditions of personal engagement and disengagement at work', *Academy of Management Review*, 33(4): 692–724.

Ouchi, W. G. (1982) *Theory Z*. Avon Books.

Yukl, G. A. (2006) *Leadership in organizations*. Upper Saddle River, NJ: Pearson Prentice Hall.

Zohar, D. (2021) *Zero distance management in the quantum age*. Springer Nature.

Part C

Lead

It is time you considered your own leadership transformation journey. Leadership remains a nebulous concept in an interconnected world; to navigate its complexity you need a guiding philosophy. In this part of the book, we invite you to adopt a new ontology of leadership with RenDanHeYi.

Learn to lead with RenDanHeYi

Introduction

This chapter introduces the notion that the reader may need to transform into a leader who thrives in a connected organisation. Research, intimate interviews and top tips from leaders successfully leading with the RenDanHeYi (RDHY) model highlight the roles that leaders at every level can play in serving the three stakeholders of the model and in deepening the connections between all three to create long-lasting and sustainable business growth.

The need for personal transformation as a leader

We find it interesting that despite several books written on the subject of leadership, the concept of leadership remains largely elusive and its definition is equally nebulous. In fact, one of the most prominent leadership scholars of the twentieth century, Ralph Melvin Stogdill (1904–1978), famously stated that 'there are as many definitions of leadership as there are those who have attempted to define the concept'. Stogdill was among the first scholars to argue against the 'great man theory' in which it was believed that certain traits in people made them leaders. Leadership is certainly about more than traits. In this sense, we can expect an individual in a leadership position to look beyond their own personal traits and to rethink what specific behaviours they must adopt, perhaps embody, in order to lead successfully. In other words, it should be possible for a manager of an organisation to reinvent himself or herself so they can meet the present challenges posed by the ever-changing business environment. One implicit assumption that undergirds the philosophy of RDHY is the idea of the constantly changing business environment where customers are no longer 'outsiders' but freely navigate both the internal and external worlds of the organisation. Accordingly, a leader who refuses to adapt to changes occurring within the organisation as a result of the new organisational entrant – the customer – will ultimately fail.

This argument for personal transformation of leaders in the new world of work began more than four decades ago when leadership scholars started exploring theories such as transactional and transformational leadership. The works of James MacGregor Burns and Bernard Bass are particularly instructive. They moved away from leadership traits to leadership behaviours that support effective leadership. These include inspirational motivation, idealised influence, intellectual stimulation and individualised consideration. Although this shift in thinking was welcome in academic circles, the practice of leadership continued to revolve around individual charisma and traits, largely encouraged by popular culture and the media. Movies tend to celebrate individual heroism based upon charisma, grit or intellect. The reach of the print media is also now accelerated by digital media as stories of heroic achievements of individual leaders spread far and wide. While this focus on individual heroics is not necessarily a bad thing, as people deserve to be recognised for their achievements, the flip side is that what we celebrate in leaders is often carefully constructed or curated for public consumption. The implication is that 'consumers' of leadership can be deceived into the wrong ideals of what leadership is all about.

For a connected organisation, managers must look beyond themselves. In fact, the network of actors working within the organisation all carry the ability to influence one another. Leadership within contemporary organisations is therefore a multidirectional phenomenon and no one singular individual must seek to become the centre of attention. This shift in thinking about what defines leadership has implications for managers. An understanding of leadership as multidirectional means that it is not about the position held within the organisation, but about the influence exerted. In practice, a junior colleague may carry higher leadership influence than a senior individual in a managerial position. To lead requires personal transformation in order to be effective. This transformation is one that acknowledges that there are various other actors with interconnections within the organisation. These individuals act on each other in various ways: employees acting on managers and vice versa; customers acting on employees and vice versa; the organisation acting on both managers and employees and vice versa. This requires managers to think in terms of networks and ecosystems, and to avoid the self-absorbed notions of who a leader is, which only leads to hubris. The human-centric notion of RDHY is a call for leaders to transform into individuals who serve others and help others achieve their highest potentials. This personal transformation is what makes leadership possible in an RDHY-practising organisation.

Thriving in a connected organisation

The principle of RDHY is underpinned by the idea that all members of an ecosystem work together in a way that sustains each as well as the whole. This means that members of organisations in the ecosystem understand that there is an interdependence that defines and frames their relationships. Recognising and working in an interdependent manner helps to address the potentially dysfunctional aspects of functional specialisation, which is often the hallmark of formal organisational structures. These include destructive internal dynamics, unhealthy rivalry and competition as well as silo mentality. For instance, the Internet of Food (IoF) is an ecosystem that is made up of several complementary parts and actors, including chefs, customers, farmers and other participants within the value chain. Each of these actors feeds into the activities of others to keep the ecosystem functioning. For example, while farmers provide the raw material in terms of foodstuff, experienced chefs are able to utilise their expertise in producing recipes that are appealing to the final customer who is the consumer of the meal.

In order to thrive within work relationships underpinned by the RDHY principle, three key things are necessary: understanding collective value and shared cognition, shared value systems and a willingness to seek the common good. An ecosystem is made up of different members with diverse abilities and resources. Having shared knowledge and an understanding of the value that each member of the ecosystem brings to the table is key to sustaining connections and growing the ecosystem. Having a shared understanding of the collective resources available in an ecosystem allows for decisions to be made regarding opportunities that present themselves for growth and deeper collaboration. Decision-making becomes faster, as all members operate as nodes that simultaneously interact with the environment and make sense of the information obtained in ways that benefit the wider ecosystem. Second, there is a need for shared value systems that guide members and act as an informal moral compass, as depicted in Figure 6.1. Rather than competitive internal rivalry and exploitation, the ecosystem is characterised by shared goals, mutual support and dependence, and collaboration. This shared value system is particularly important because it is the glue that binds members of the ecosystem together, irrespective of their function or needs. Third, there must be a willingness of all members to seek the common good of the ecosystem. This comes from the understanding that what affects one part will eventually affect others within the ecosystem. In this sense, each member becomes a custodian of the culture of interdependence such that everyone is focused on performing at their best, with the knowledge that a supporting system is behind them.

Within an organisation connected by the principle of RDHY, three key actors can be identified: organisational leaders, customers and employees. Each of these plays a role in the continued existence of the ecosystem and works independently with others for collective benefit. Customers are not a homogeneous group, as they may cover a range of industries or sectors. Similarly, employees are used to refer broadly to those formally in the employment of the organisation. For the purpose of analysis, however, it is useful to discuss these different categories in turn as dyads. This approach allows us to conduct a deeper analysis of the intricacies and nuances in the relationships, thereby reaching a deeper understanding of the connected organisation.

The role of leadership in serving the customer

Leadership is often viewed conventionally in terms of the relationship of influence between two parties – leaders and followers. Traditional conceptions of leadership have focused on several aspects of people on the basis of which they are then identified as leaders. This is often an emphasis on physical traits and abilities that are

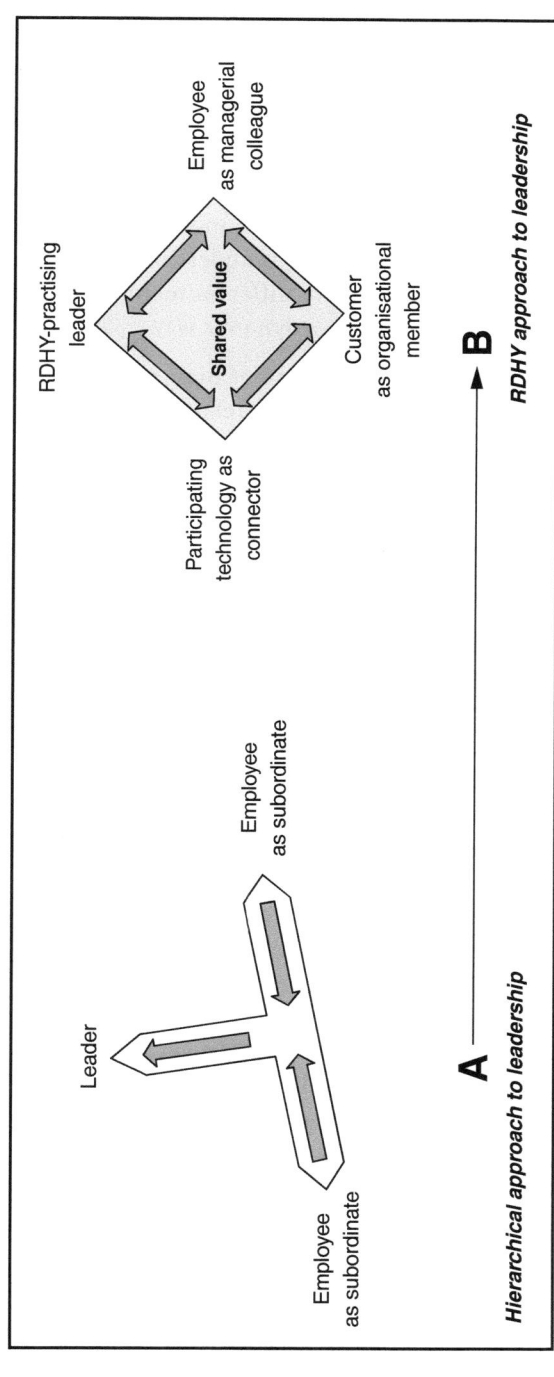

Figure 6.1 Transitioning from hierarchical to an RDHY approach to leadership.

observed in a person, a person's concern for tasks or for people, or the idea that leadership could be seen to emerge as a result of particular situations, in which case leadership is said to be situational. More critical perspectives see leadership as not being vested in one particular individual but as situated within relationships or as being distributed or shared. This perspective takes the focus away from a single individual to a more diffuse notion of leadership. The RDHY principle is best understood in terms of this latter notion of leadership, where different members of an ecosystem take on leadership roles in a dynamic way.

By upturning traditional ideas of hierarchy and authority, distributed leadership allows for a relatively flatter organisational structure such that power and influence become multidirectional. Against this backdrop, it is possible to introduce non-traditional participants such as customers into the leadership space. With a distributed notion of leadership, we can have direct connections between organisational leaders and customers. As explained, the customers do not operate as conventional 'followers' who obey the leader without question, but they exist as co-creators of value in a mutually beneficial relationship. This is of value to the organisation as well as to the customer. Furthermore, the orientation to the customer in this type of relationship is one of service, whereby a leader in an organisation shares the same collaborative perspective of the relationship. In the absence of traditional notions of power, authority and organisational boundaries, the leader's relationship with the customer is underpinned by an understanding of customer needs as well as the skills and capabilities which can benefit the ecosystem. This mutually beneficial relationship creates fairly blurred organisational boundaries in both physical and cognitive terms, where the customer has free access to organisational spaces, ideas and strategic activities. Haier provides a good example of such shared organisational spaces in the way that it allows its customers access to its manufacturing plants and actively involves them in the design and development process. The thinking behind this approach is that the customer represents a key source of strategic input for the sustainability of the business and the ecosystem.

It is also worth noting that there is an interconnectedness across key participants in an ecosystem, whereby the output from one becomes the input for another, and several groups may take on the label 'customer', depending on who is the beneficiary of their respective output. Organisations therefore have 'open' boundaries. This type of openness presupposes that there is mutual trust in the relationship and a symbiotic engagement with one another in the pursuit of shared goals. Serving a customer means that leaders have the customer's needs and interests at the heart of business decision-making. It is a truly customer-centric approach which 'walks the talk'. Many organisations pay lip service to the customer, while in reality the dominant orientation is that of instrumentality, where the customer serves as a rational means to an end. RDHY allows for a redefinition of such organisational 'ends' in more collaborative terms. In addition, it creates opportunities for co-developing the most appropriate ways to achieve shared goals. This approach preserves the dignity of both parties (leader and customer) as human beings while allowing them to work and thrive together. Leadership plays an important role in framing the terms of this connected relationship and ensuring that there is organisational buy-in. The journey to becoming a connected organisation begins as a process and it is the role of leaders, in the sense that we have defined them, to communicate a clear direction of travel in terms of goals and how to reach those goals.

The role of leadership in serving employees

Another perspective of the leader's relationship within a connected organisation has to do with employees. Similar to the conventional notion of the power structure in a typical formal organisation, employees can be said to occupy a subordinate position to leaders at different organisational levels. In recent times, the dynamics of relations in organisations have experienced a shift, whereby employees are now more vocal, more demanding and, like customers, have greater expectations when it comes to employers and the condition surrounding how they work. Research shows that this shift has been accelerated by the COVID-19 pandemic, as employees increasingly prioritise work–life balance and flexibility, which makes them consider leaving jobs they are unhappy with to seek out jobs that offer these. What this dynamic reveals is that the power structure has experienced a shift and employees have greater leverage in the organisation. Against this background, it is incumbent upon leaders in organisations to pay close attention to how they can create value for employees. Better still, there needs to be a clear focus on working collaboratively with employees to meet organisational goals in a way that also addresses employee needs.

While organisational goals are often articulated publicly on company websites, literature and in advertisements or public relations campaigns, employee needs are less easy to identify. Beyond basic needs, Herzberg, a renowned management scholar, has published work on what motivates workers and identifies what he calls 'hygiene factors' and 'motivators'. Hygiene factors are those important things without which employees would be dissatisfied, e.g. salary. These factors have been found to be linked to employee productivity and, in turn, organisational performance. While salary, relationships with supervisors, colleagues and peers form basic hygiene factors without which employees will be dissatisfied, motivators include recognition of achievement, higher levels of responsibility, as well as opportunities for advancement and growth. Herzberg's research establishes that it is the motivators that drive productivity in employees. The principle of RDHY that underpins business ecosystems in Haier offers a means to align organisational goals with employee needs in a way that moves beyond lip service. Employees at Haier are encouraged to seek personal and professional growth through leading enterprise micro-communities. Such micro-leadership roles create a positive environment for intrapreneurship, as employees leverage their entrepreneurial skills to develop and grow new businesses or product lines, even though they are still in formal employment. The experience of building and working with small teams in the ecosystem micro-communities (EMCs) provides opportunities for meeting the employees' higher-order needs and simultaneously expanding the frontiers of the organisation. Leadership that serves employees is one that recognises the intrinsic value of employees, not simply as expendable resources but as organisational partners in progress. Business models that share this perspective of partnership create conditions for autonomy but also interdependence towards increasing productivity. They include professional services firms like accounting, law and architectural firms where leadership is diffused and a team of partners drives the business. By contrast, EMCs and the ecosystems that nurture them have more flexible organisational boundaries that allow for organic growth and simultaneously provide motivating factors for enriching employee performance. Serving employees therefore involves a shift in conventional managerial thinking and placing employee needs at the heart of organisational decision-making.

Deepening the connections across the three stakeholders

As we have alluded to so far, management is simply not about metrics or the bottom line. It is not so much the idea that 'what gets measured gets managed', but also that 'what can't be measured must be managed', as famed management scholar Henry Mintzberg would often argue. It is difficult to measure how close customers are to the organisation. It is even harder to measure how close customers are to employees. In fact, the thought of bringing customers and employees closer is not what is taught at our Western universities. We might come across the idea of bringing customers closer to an organisation and we might discuss issues surrounding branding, customer loyalty, customer feedback and so on at our universities. But to bring customers and employees closer? That sounds alien! We might feel that way because the traditional conceptualisation of the customer is one who is there to 'consume' what's on offer but must be wooed to do so. It is almost a game of using bait to catch a fish. For instance, organisations would offer discount codes, design and showcase glamorous pop-up stores for quick sales, arrange flash mobs, issue loyalty cards, conduct raffles with the promise of attractive prizes, and many more! The underlying assumption is that the customer is 'out there' with a fickle desire, doesn't know what they want and can be easily driven away to a competitor. This view of the customer makes it difficult to think of a scenario in which a connection between employees and customers exists, let alone deepening that connection.

The philosophy of RDHY possesses a worldview that does not separate Napoleons from commoners. Its human-centric approach holds the customer in as high esteem as it holds the employee. Accordingly, the view of the customer as outside the organisation does not hold. This fundamental shift (as we showed in Chapter 4) is needed so that the customer would not be seen as a 'consumer' but as one who uses the services or products of the organisation. Innovation scholar Clayton Christensen (1952–2020) argued that the customer must be seen as one who 'hires' a product or a service from an organisation. As one 'hiring' a product, the customer considers what 'job' the product or service would do for them. In other words, customers are not mere 'consumers', there to take what is on offer to satisfy their hunger. Should that be the case, anything on offer must suffice as they would be at the mercy of the organisation. In fact, they should be grateful that anything is on offer at all, just as the wise proverb goes that 'to the hungry man, every bitter thing is sweet'. A hungry 'consumer' would therefore not need to be brought closer to the employee for any reason other than to receive an offering; forget the idea of a value proposition, they must simply accept anything without a choice.

From the arguments raised so far, we can see how organisations that do not make this fundamental shift in how they think about customers risk losing them. The point is simple: the customer and the employee must be valued equally, their opinions respected, their inputs brought to the decision table of the organisation, worked with daily as we would with employees, engaged with continuously, and managed with empathy as we would with employees. This is at the heart of an RDHY organisation and it calls for a deepening of the connections between all elements of the model, i.e. the customer, the employee and the organisation (see Figure 2.2).

In deepening the connection among these three stakeholders, the participating technology is crucial. Organisations could leverage available technologies in enhancing these connections (as we established in Chapter 4). What we wish to emphasise here is the role of the participating technology. In a hyper-connected world, the digital technologies at play are not simply there as tools to be used to do a job. The old instrumentalist view of technology worked in the previous industrial revolutions. In the first industrial revolution, technology helped move manual labour to something mechanical. In the second industrial revolution, we observed a move to the conveyor belt, and technology helped us to standardise production and increase in output. The third industrial revolution was the age of computing and we witnessed computers helping us to achieve so much more than we thought was ever possible. All these eras still held the notion that technologies could help humans do things they would not be able to do by themselves or do them in a much more efficient manner.

In recent times, characterised by the fourth industrial revolution, we have observed something quite unique. Technology is no longer just a tool we use; it has become part of our lives. We wake up each morning with technology beside our beds and in some cases the entire home is connected through the Internet of Things (IoT). The ubiquitous smartphone has brought digital technology to every aspect of our lives, including the work lives of employees. By default, the opportunities for establishing a connection between employees and customers already exist as digital technology permeates society. This current era of the fourth industrial revolution introduces connectivity in ways that were not thought possible before. For instance, it is relatively easy to connect devices and people. Various sensors built into devices (and, in some cases, into tech-enhanced humans) make connectivity between human and non-human elements seamless. The smartphone is no longer a tool for making a phone call but is now an extension of the self, carrying with it everything there is to know about its owner. In the extreme cases of individuals who have enhanced themselves with technology implants, connectivity is now even more personal and embodied. This era therefore makes the customer–employee connectivity question a foregone conclusion; in other words, if the organisation doesn't make it happen, it will happen (or is already happening) anyway.

To deepen the connection among the three stakeholders – the organisation, employee and customer – the understanding of technology as a participating element of the triad must be translated into something practical. This calls for investment in specific platform technologies that ensure that customers have access and voice within the organisation. At the same time, this open access must ensure that employees are able to interact freely with the customer, working with the customer, not simply chatting to the customer. This is not merely a game of listening to customer needs; that can be done in conventional ways of customer surveys and focus groups and various other market research techniques. In deepening the connection, we mean bringing the voice of the customer to bear on how the organisation operates and what offerings are provided. This allows employees to engage creatively with customers and to ensure that the product or service offerings are indeed tailored to the needs of the customer.

Creating sustainable business growth

Our focus in this chapter is to highlight the importance and significance of a connected organisation, where customers, employees and the organisation are interdependent collaborators. This connection is the foundation for business growth, as customers become key sources of new ideas, products or product developments. Working collaboratively to uncover customer needs (both current and future) creates limitless opportunities for company growth, as the company evolves with its customers and remains relevant through time. Apart from the customer, other members of the ecosystem represent potential sources of strategic input into business decision-making. As a result, EMCs are able to achieve growth through a deep understanding of their target markets. Additionally, as customers evolve in their preferences and their needs change, there are opportunities for future markets to be developed. Many factors can influence changing customer needs and preferences. These include emerging needs related to age, gender, changing priorities and values, shifting social discourses which lead to changes in preferences, the impact of technological advances and information communication technologies, as well as the role of social media as a catalyst for societal change.

A strong understanding of the profiles of current customers, as well as how these evolve, provides a rich source of data that the organisation can mine to reveal the direction of customer preferences and needs. Keeping close connections between the organisation and customers enables a timely response to changing customer needs such that customer satisfaction and customer loyalty are preserved. Haier is keen to expand the RDHY practice in its EMCs, and its piloting of the EMC idea led to development of its IoT, which, over time, has contributed to building its brand image. The brand image has thus been transformed from a traditional product brand to an ecosystem brand. Examples of EMCs within the IoT include the Internet of Food. These structures not only inspire the potential of ecosystem partners but also incentivise participants in the ecosystem. As a result, a pathway for healthy competition as well as healthy and sustainable growth is created for enterprises within the ecosystem. Research indicates that Haier's ecosystem has pulled in over 1500 brands and almost 10,000 ecosystem partners globally. Additionally, over 1,100 internal entrepreneurs have been created with value-added returns. Despite a lull in the home appliances industry in major global markets, Haier was able to achieve growth as a result of its ecosystem model.

Practising leaders of the RDHY philosophy emphasise the role of this close connection to the customer and suggest that core values of equality, dignity and autonomy are key constituents of the practice. These values ensure that resources are provided and employees are empowered to grow as individuals but also as entrepreneurs. This approach represents an expression of Haier's corporate management paradigm, which aims to maximise human value. The organisational structure of EMCs is one major way that autonomy is built into the design of work. Three types of microenterprises characterise the Internet of Things. There are user microenterprises, node microenterprises and a shared services platform. User microenterprises mainly interact with customers or end-users in order to address their needs. They maintain open communication channels to uncover current and future customer needs to which the organisation can respond. Node microenterprises emerged from the splitting of supporting platforms such as supply chain, R&D and logistics. User and node microenterprises work collaboratively in a networked structure and operate on the basis of contracts that define financial obligations. The third type of microenterprise, the shared services platform, describes former functional departments that have been integrated into a common platform and provide services to both user and node microenterprises. Functional departments that merged into a single shared services platform include human resources, legal, information technology services and finance, which all work together to serve the microenterprises.

By converting siloed and functionally organised departments into a shared platform which provides operational support via software and relevant operational systems, traditional organisational barriers are broken down to create a seamless and connected organisation. The results of Haier's performance have thus shown the value of its approach to organisational structure. By inverting the Japanese-style traditional bureaucracy, where there are increasingly fewer formal leaders as one moves towards the top of the pyramid than in the opposite direction, Haier has fuelled a new era of ownership and autonomy, simultaneously providing impetus for employee motivation and sustained performance as it seeks to fulfil its purpose of maximising human value. From our research of Haier, we find that the 'Internet of Air' represents a good example of how deepening the connections between the key players in the ecosystems can contribute to sustainable performance and business growth (see Case Study 6.1).

Case Study 6.1

Haier's Internet of Air

Haier air conditioners (ACs) is a popular brand within the broader Haier Group and was established in 1985. The Haier Group is the foremost white goods manufacturer and a valuable brand in China repositioning itself in the smart fresh air solutions space and focusing on 'making fresh air' as opposed to 'making good air conditioners'.

Industry reports and market research from Euromonitor International, the world's leading market research agency, indicate that between 2017 and 2019, Haier showed sustained performance in its market and was ranked among the top independent Chinese brands in terms of export of household AC brands. Its market share ranged from 30.9% to 40.7%. Haier has been associated with many firsts in this industry and shaped the market for ACs in China, developing the first split AC, the first inverter, the first multi-split AC, the first fluorine-free inverter AC and the first energy-saving direct-current inverter. Following the trends in ecosystem development, Haier created the first IoT AC, followed by other innovative products, including launching a mixed fresh air technology, which uses an air tunnel design to integrate cold and ambient air such that the resultant air is at an optimum temperature. In step with its vision to 'make fresh air', this innovation also offers a self-cleaning technology which allows the AC to self-clean.

Systematically, Haier expanded its product range through innovative technology and continuous improvement to create various solutions for its customers. For instance, through engagement

> with customers, it added an air-purifier technology to the self-cleaning AC to clean indoor air and also moved into the smart wearable space by designing a smart watch which allows voice commands to control ACs. Haier has also been part of the conversation on setting industry standards for the installation of several products by working with regulatory authorities. In this instance, the company opened its doors and shared some proprietary technologies with its peers to enable shared progress while also building its own ecosystem of collaborative organisations. For instance, collaborations with Apple produced a mutually beneficial relationship, as Apple named Haier its global home appliances partner.

The actions described in the case study demonstrate the openness and ecosystem thinking that underpin the RDHY management philosophy that permeates organisational life in our study organisation. There is a lot to learn here. The goal of bringing customers closer has led Haier to place emphasis on R&D and has thus established research centres in several countries such as New Zealand, Germany, Japan, China and the US. This has created opportunities for expanding its reach and innovative capabilities while integrating local resources into its production activities. With its 18 manufacturing facilities around the world – nine in China and nine in other countries – Haier positioned itself to respond to consumer demand in a timely manner in a way that minimises supply disruption or stock shortages. Haier's central research institute has 46 laboratories that specialise in technologies for environmental simulation, noise and EMCs. The central research institute works with five R&D centres to generate a suite of advanced technologies that advance the AC industry. In its usual partnership approach to development, Haier and Honeywell established a joint innovation centre to conduct research on household appliances and intelligent control based on decarbonisation, reduction in emissions and efficiency gains. This initiative was taken as a response to customer sentiments as the organisation engages with its customers to bring their needs to the decision-making table. Another joint laboratory was established with Shanghai Hitachi and Mitsubishi Electric to produce compressors, semiconductor chips, refrigeration and heat pump technologies, among others. This partnership allows Haier's partners to leverage their respective strengths in pursuing cutting-edge technology and innovation within the AC industry.

When it comes to product design, Haier integrates a deep understanding of its customers. For instance, it unveiled Tianzun, a smart AC which was well received and voted as users' choice AC in 2014. Other products include the Tianbo AC, Dizun AC, Air Box and Air Mini. These products represent a turn towards intelligent technologies in the industry but, more importantly, are outcomes of its close collaboration with customers. As an example, Haier introduced a smart AC for young people in 2015 to meet the younger generation's need for a smart experience. While delivering what customers want, Haier focused on meeting the need for fresh air rather than just an AC and launched the idea of a fresh air ecosystem. This included a partnership with China Building Material Test & Certification Group (CTC) and Weather China in order to establish the Healthy Air Ecosystem Alliance. The idea of the fresh air ecosystem attracted over 500 fresh air resource providers and was embraced by the industry and other brands which also started developing their own ecosystems for fresh air solutions.

As leaders in the ecosystem, Haier stayed ahead of competitors as it leveraged its close relationship with customers to create solutions for specific user groups. For example, the company created solutions for mothers and babies, university campuses and other corporate clients by reinventing its business model to add fresh air solutions for these customer segments. An AC sharing solution, for instance, has been useful for universities and this solution has been replicated in over 300 institutions of higher learning across China. In its study of user habits, Haier also deploys technology for autonomous detection, decisioning and processing to create scenario-based customisation. These simulations allow the design of personalised air solutions, including for outdoor grassland, living room and bedroom spaces. These technologies are considered as part of the process and not simply tools that are used to achieve an end. As a result, their use is highly focused on fulfilling customer needs, in this case 'making fresh air'.

Unsurprisingly, Haier's business performance shows success in sales and exports, as well as a strong brand in electronics with accolades in energy efficiency rated by the United States Environmental Protection Agency (EPA) and EUROVENT. The approach of Haier to product development and internationalisation reflects a shift from a hardware era, where the product is regarded as king, to a new ecosystem era where employees work with customers to deliver value. By bringing together a wide range of resource providers, knowledge and resources are shared and integrated within the ecosystem. The key thinking underpinning the partnerships built is one in which co-creation and collaboration drive innovation and creativity. This value generated by an ecosystem would otherwise not be available to a single organisation. By opening up the boundaries of the organisation, opportunities for jointly envisioning the future of the fresh air ecosystem are created. In this sense, ecosystem partners leverage platform capabilities and channel openness and sharing, all of which illustrate the core values of the RDHY philosophy. The ecosystem allows resource providers to operate not as silos but as partners who share a common focus on the AC and its development to meet user needs. They thus think in terms of solutions for all spaces inhabited by users such as the home, office, commercial spaces, mobility etc., as well as a variety of lifestyle scenarios which enable the creation of a personalised fresh air experience for users. Through challenging conventional ideas about organisational structure, organisational boundaries and organisational values, Haier is thus able to achieve its objectives through co-creation, which involves a close collaboration between its employees and customers with participating technology at the core of the relationship.

Leading successfully with the RenDanHeYi model

The human-centric approach to management that underscores the philosophy of RDHY is one that is rooted in a collaborative leadership style. To lead successfully with the RDHY triad (see Figure 2.2), managers must begin to re-examine their own leadership styles critically. This calls for reflexive actions upon self-examination. Directive approaches to leadership must give way to concepts such as delegation, which, as we argued in our paper 'Embrace delegation as a skill to strengthen remote teams', must be an embodied skill, not simply something managers do as part of their jobs. From Case Study 6.1, it is evident that success is often achieved collaboratively – in this case, collaborative efforts among all stakeholders involved, not sole decisions made from the organisation alone.

However, these things are not without their challenges. Working collaboratively comes with its own messy situations. The organisation must think carefully about its own internal capabilities and employees would often think about the amount of resources or time needed to execute what customers want while bearing in mind other demanding customers or tasks to be done. This juggling act requires skill, negotiation and trade-offs. It would be easier for an organisation to design a product it has the internal capability for, which the customer then purchases, than to engage with often conflicting voices from customers. However, RDHY wants the organisation to look outside of its own interests and fulfil the needs of the human, not simply design a product or service and sell it. In this sense, we find RDHY-practising organisations, as shown in Haier's AC unit, not only seeking to make good ACs but exploring and addressing the needs of the human with such a purpose as 'making fresh air'. Surely, the organisation is not under any illusion as to actually make fresh air, but its reconceptualisation of the *raison d'être* ensures consistency with its management philosophy. Of course, this may or may not translate into actual performance on the ground for some organisations that simply have a tagline for its own sake. The key is to ensure that the practice of management within the organisation can be matched to the espoused values.

The gaps in what is said versus what is done is a potential limitation in terms of organisations deploying RDHY management principles. This is where leadership becomes crucial in driving change. A study by management scholars Amal Ahmadi and Lebene Soga in 2022 on entrepreneurial behaviour showed that fear can be more of an inhibiting factor to wanting to do something than to actually doing it. Interestingly, the study also argues that fear can be a driving force towards actually doing something. This demonstrates the importance of contextual elements dictating whether individuals or an organisation takes on the challenge of this human-centric approach to management, which has evidently transformed companies like Haier, Sanyo and GE Appliances, or whether they shy away from it through fear. Leading successfully with RDHY is possible. However, we warn that walking that road places a demand on you as a manager. It is a transformational demand on your management style where you take on humility, devolve power and invite your employees and customers to take on leadership. Those who relish being the centre of attention cannot lead with RDHY. It is those who genuinely seek to transform and make an impact who are able to take advantage of the transformative power of the philosophy of RDHY.

Chapter summary, reflective questions and practical implications

One consistent theme among managers we studied is their belief in autonomy and collaborative practice. For instance, the head of Haier Japan would often visit his staff for a drink and for informal conversations. Employees speak of how they find these moments necessary for passing on their thoughts to their leader. Japan is known for its high power distance and this approach by managers in this cultural context runs counter to what their contemporaries in other organisations are used to. The courage to do things differently is another important tip from several managers we spoke to. This sounds almost like a cliché, but it really takes courage to practise what they preach. The key here is to ensure the narrative of what RDHY is all about is consistent throughout the organisation and to stick to its ideals. It is like wearing a lens through which everyone sees. We observe this in societies where cultural artefacts have meaning that is consistent among the tribe. The same can be replicated within the organisation where RDHY becomes a 'cultural' organisational lens for meaning-making. Another tip for managers is to open the door for 'outsiders' and to keep that door open. This includes building one's own value chain within the ecosystem. For instance, the analogy used by former chairman of Haier, Zhang Ruimin, is that of the rainforest. As a forest, it is open to the emergence of all fauna and flora who all play a role in sustaining it. Similarly, being open means working collaboratively with other organisations within the ecosystem instead of competing with them. For example, it makes sense for a smart kitchen business to work closely with the furniture production company or with the local restaurants or food nutritionists, and so on. While some of these collaborations are the common-sense things to do, sometimes such openness must be actively worked out and built with intentionality. The pro tip here is to actively seek out those within your ecosystem who can help deliver your value proposition as an organisation and to build that connection. Finally, managers that excel with RDHY are adventurous in their use of technology. They see technology as a necessary element of their day-to-day activities and seek new ways of engaging with customers. A pro tip here is to use what you already have more creatively in engaging, instead of simply disseminating. Your social media platforms alone can be used a bit more strategically to build a sense of belonging with your customers instead of merely speaking at them.

In summary, here are some reflective questions and practical ideas you can adopt to help you lead with the RDHY approach:

- *How open are you to delegation and sharing power?* Encourage autonomy and collaborative practice. You can do this by devolving power as you break down hierarchies, assign new roles and create teams that are tasked with building an EMC.

- *How are your previous notions about management and leadership preventing you from embracing change?* Have the courage to challenge your preconceived notions about management and do things differently. You can do this by casting a new vision in your next management meeting and inviting others to join you on this journey. Change is possible. A quick and useful template for your vision casting could include the following: *story* – share the story of where you have come from to where you are now; *statement* – provide an aspirational statement of where you want to be; *slogan* – capture what must be done in a memorable way; and *steps* – provide actionable steps that individuals must follow to get to where you want to be. Vision-casting is done successfully when it is done collaboratively, thus ensuring corporate ownership.

- *What new relationships within your ecosystem could be built for your organisation's goals?* Actively seek out those within your ecosystem who can help you deliver value, and work collaboratively with them to build your value chain. You can do this by copying the EMC model we discussed earlier (see Chapter 2). Let your employees build new connections and you will find value in them.

- *Could your current technology be used any differently?* With respect to technology, start by using the platforms you already have more creatively to engage your employees and customers. Sometimes it is simply about how the technology is used instead of investing in something new altogether.

Bibliography

Ahmadi, A. & Soga, L. R. (2022) 'To be or not to be: latent entrepreneurship, the networked agent and the fear factor', *Technological Forecasting and Social Change*, 174, doi: https://doi.org/10.1016/j.techfore.2021.121281

Alade, K., Windapo, A. & Wachira, T. I. N. (2021) 'Rethinking leadership in the fourth industrial revolution: lessons for construction business organizations', *Journal of Leadership Studies*, 15(1): 74–80.

Bass, B. M. (1985) 'Leadership: good, better, best', *Organizational Dynamics*, 13(3): 26–40.

Bass, B. M. (1999) 'Two decades of research and development in transformational leadership'. *European Journal of Work and Organizational Psychology*, 8(1): 9–32.

Burns, J. M. (2004) *Transformational leadership.* Grove Press.

Christensen, C. (1997) *The innovator's dilemma.* Harvard Business Review Press.

Drucker, P. F. (1999) *Management challenges for the 21st century.* Elsevier Ltd.

Gronn, P. (2002) 'Distributed leadership as a unit of analysis', *The Leadership Quarterly*, 13(4), pp. 423–451.

Gronn, P. (2008) 'The future of distributed leadership', *Journal of Educational Administration*, 46(2): 141–158.

Hackman, J. R., Oldham, G. R. (1976) 'Motivation through the design of work: test of a theory', *Organizational Behavior and Human Performance*, 16(2): 250–279.

Herzberg, F. (1966) *Work and the nature of man.* Cleveland, OH: World Publishing.

Herzberg, F. (1968) 'One more time: how do you motivate employees?', *Harvard Business Review*, 46(1): 53–62.

Mintzberg, H. (2009) *Managing*. FT Press.

Moss, J. (2022) 'The pandemic changed us. Now companies have to change too', *Harvard Business Review*, available at https://hbr.org/2022/07/the-pandemic-changed-us-now-companies-have-to-change-too (accessed 19 August 2022).

Soga, L., Laker, B., Bolade-Ogunfodun, Y. & Mariani, M. (2021) 'Embrace delegation as a skill to strengthen remote teams', *MIT Sloan Management Review*, 63 (1): 1–3.

Stogdill, R. M. (1974) *Handbook of leadership: a survey of theory and research*, 2nd edition. Publisher Free Press.

Serve more than just the customer

Introduction

This chapter suggests that readers look beyond the ever-popular concept of 'servant leadership' (by which a leader's primary goal is to serve others above themselves) to a new form of leadership more compatible with working in a connected ecosystem. We will discuss the traits and skills of a leader who can realistically serve customers and employees as well as the organisation, all without compromising on their resilience or the company's financial situation. The two forms of leadership are compared side by side before providing you with practical ideas from successful leaders for personal and professional development.

The value of servant leadership

Leadership as a practice has remained a conceptually difficult thing for both managers and academics. Our failure first of all to define what it is makes practising it something hard to grasp. Various forms of leadership have emerged over the years and the several books written about the concept are not something we can enumerate here. It has been defined in many ways and we do not wish to add to what is already a saturated space of definitions of leadership. In fact, leadership scholars Warren Bennis and Burt Nanus conducted a study[1] to see how leadership has been defined over the years and found more than 850 definitions of leadership in the extant literature! We can only assume how that figure has increased over the two decades since their study was conducted as we write this book. This is not surprising for us or other scholars in the field because of the complexity of what it means to lead in human societies and how to research it. An important scholar in the field of leadership, Keith Grint,[2] states that 'leadership research appears to be anything but incremental in its approach to "the truth" about leadership: the longer we spend looking at leadership the more complex the picture becomes'.

On the basis that leadership can be an elusive concept, we carefully navigate what we mean by servant leadership as we talk about serving more than just the customer in this chapter. Arguably, servant leadership is one of those several name tags that leadership carries but we try to make this as practical as possible and argue for managers to go beyond this idea of leadership alone. First of all, what is servant leadership all about? Two key figures are often mentioned in the literature when you read about servant leadership. You don't have to look far to come across Florence Nightingale and Mother Theresa as exemplars of servant leadership in the way they cared for the sick, their humility, their compassion and their selflessness. This is a great way of understanding servant leadership but there is a lot more to it. It was Robert Greenleaf[3] who first proposed this notion of servant leadership, although elements of this concept have long been present in the extant literature. Greenleaf's idea of servant leadership was inspired by Hermann Hesse's 1932 classic *A Journey to the East*, a novel in which a group of individuals called 'The League' embark on a pilgrimage to the East in their spiritual search for the 'ultimate truth'. The treacherous journey is made easy as they are guided and supported by Leo, a simple 'servant', but whose disappearance along the way throws the league into complete disarray so that the entire pilgrimage is ultimately abandoned. In their disappointment at the failure of the mission, seemingly due to the disappearance of Leo, a member of the league makes an effort to find answers. This search for meaning is satisfied after he eventually meets up with Leo only to find out that Leo the servant is in reality the leader of the league who commissioned the entire spiritual quest. It is this revelation of the 'servant' as 'leader' that underpins Greenleaf's idea of servant leadership. It is the idea that the leader is not necessarily one holding a high position or possessing a big title but someone who is able to serve those they lead.

From that perspective of one who serves others, leadership takes on a new meaning. It signals certain behaviours that would be characterised as servant-like, for example, one who is humble, unquestioning, compassionate, altruistic, kind, endearing, and so on. This has value to both leaders and employees alike as these behaviours create an atmosphere that is supportive and which generates commitment to the organisation. However, in reality, people might expect a leader to be compassionate or kind but not one who would gird themselves with a towel to wash the feet of those they lead. What servant leaders do in organisations, therefore, might take different forms or behavioural patterns but it ultimately places those being served first. It is akin to what leadership author Simon Sinek argues in his book, *Leaders Eat Last,* a theme of servanthood aptly captured in the title. However, in Greenleaf's view, servant leadership could have a dark side when the leader uses 'service' as a tool for manipulation. In other words, an individual could deploy servant leadership with purely selfish aims. Accordingly, it should be considered as the 'servant leader' as portrayed in Hesse's *A Journey to the East,* as opposed to 'leader servant'. In the case of the former, the servant is the one at the heart of leadership; that is, the individual is first a servant at heart who then goes on to lead others. In the case of the latter, the individual is not a servant at heart but uses 'servanthood' as a tool with which to lead others. This fundamental difference poses a challenge for the practice of servant leadership in that it is almost indistinguishable as to what or who an individual in leadership really is. In this light, we challenge managers to look beyond this notion of servant leadership alone and to consider the bigger picture of their organisation's context.

Looking beyond servant leadership

We have addressed the main differences between traditional forms of leadership and servant leadership. While servant leadership is focused on serving organisational members, more traditional perspectives on leadership emphasise authority, power and performance, all connected to a focal person. Servant leadership takes attention from the leader to the people to be served and aims to inspire and motivate others to grow as individuals, and creates an environment in which people can flourish.

Despite its merits, servant leadership alone does not give the full picture. Organisations operate in highly dynamic environments which sometimes require different approaches to leadership. Several actors in the environment are themselves also responding to changes in their operational spaces. Within an ecosystem framework, there are constant moving parts which may make it difficult to operate with 100% certainty all the time. In such instances, there is a need to look beyond only a trait-based approach to leadership, as situations may emerge that favour particular approaches.[4] Fiedler's 1967 contingency model of leadership is one that tries to set out a situational approach to leadership. It involves assessing different dimensions of the environment to determine how best an individual's leadership style fits the context. The elements of the environment that predispose situations to being categorised as favourable or unfavourable are the structure of the task, the position power of the leader and the relations between leader and organisational members. In the case of an ecosystem, we can extend this to relations between members of the wider ecosystem. Similarly, Tanenbaum and Schmidt's[5] 1973 continuum moves away from a static view of leadership to a dynamic one which tries to distinguish between boss-centred and subordinate-centred leadership practices. The servant leadership approach could be said to align with subordinate-centred leadership, which allows for different degrees of autonomy for organisational members.

A dynamic operating environment provides a strong impetus for firms to look beyond servant leadership. This environment can be described as having four key elements: volatility, uncertainty, complexity and ambiguity (VUCA). This creates highly unpredictable competitive environments for leaders and a myriad challenges. The change also relates to employees themselves. A number of factors contribute to a shift in the behaviours and attitudes of employees. The rise of social media platforms and the speed of global information dissemination have created opportunities for changes in thinking on a large scale. This means that an event happening in one part of the world, i.e. in India, Europe or China, could have ripple effects throughout the rest of the world. This spatial or geographic interconnectedness through technology amplifies the impact of ideas and social narratives. For example, information shared via social media platforms can go viral in a matter of seconds as people continue to spread it within their social and professional networks. Changing attitudes to work and a greater pursuit of flexible working practices have been enabled by the amplification of ideas through technology. Similarly, organisations can leverage technology to reach, communicate with and respond to a generation of users who otherwise may not have been easily accessed. This is the generation of millennials and the younger work force of the future.

Organisations that are focused on performance can benefit from practising the RDHY philosophy by creating opportunities for their employees to develop and demonstrate growth mindsets. Running ecosystem micro-communities (EMCs) is one such opportunity as it allows employees to re-envision their roles and become intrapreneurs, continually pushing the boundaries of their creative potential and playing a key role in bringing about positive multiplier effects of an integrated ecosystem. Also, pursuing growth in mainstream and peripheral sectors is key to an expansion strategy for ecosystems. This approach can then be replicated on a geographical basis by leveraging technology to understand different markets and scale production. Partnerships and strategic alliances also contribute to a growth strategy. Arguably, the ideas presented in servant leadership by Greenleaf in 1991 could not have taken into consideration the future technologically interconnected organisation or individual. In fact, we only began to see the vast possibilities afforded by the Internet over the last two decades when the Web was reconceptualised as no longer a place to simply download information from some Webmaster, but as a place to participate in the creation of information.

Leadership for an interconnected ecosystem

Recognising the interconnectedness of different sectors within ecosystems, it is evident that a leader's role extends beyond a single organisation. Given the distributed notion of leadership discussed earlier, the key actors involved in leadership are present in every part of the ecosystem. From this perspective, leadership emerges from shared goals and is underpinned by mutual trust in the relationship. Ideas for new products or modifications of existing products can come from any point in the supply chain. In this sense, the actor driving the new direction is 'leading' and others come on board by supporting the idea. For example, insights could emerge from the producer of raw materials (farmer) which could prompt an innovation in an existing product or in the business process for developing the product. The openness across traditional organisational boundaries that characterises an ecosystem creates favourable conditions for the leader's influence to permeate the entire ecosystem. As a result, open or shifting organisational boundaries expand the scope of leadership influence beyond employees and customers. The connections across the ecosystem generate, as it were, a wider organisation which operates as a network of interdependent parts without losing the identity of the constituents. Leadership in this context recognises the individuality of each component and the value of this for strengthening identity in the competitive environment. But, in addition, the operational structure is flexible and allows for a dynamic form of leadership, one that is not associated with just a single central figure.

The idea of EMCs allows any employee to take up the challenge of leadership and drive entrepreneurial activity within an organisation. In Haier, for example, employees who opt to take on such challenges are given support by the parent organisation and their micro-communities run on the technology platform of the parent company. As the EMC grows and innovates, new spin-offs are created and these in turn become new EMCs. As a result, the ecosystem expands organically while still tightly connected in terms of its ethos and the customer being served. When Haier acquired Sanyo, key changes were made in terms of the operational structure, reward systems and advancement requirements. Under a traditional leadership structure, a steep hierarchy of authority was followed and there was a waiting list for employees to advance to leadership positions. Employees had to wait for openings created when their senior colleagues retired. However, Haier established a leading goal as well as a mechanism to get employees to take responsibility. There were big goals but also smaller individual goals. In addition, the existing salary structure was broken down and tied to a new way of running the business via the RDHY principle. With RDHY, the sense of ownership shifts to everyone in the organisation, i.e. the product designers, employees, developers etc.

In this way, the performance of the company is also jointly owned, and losses are not seen as the fault of anyone in particular. This action contributes to creating psychological safety for employees and is also a source of motivation for employees to take on bigger challenges. The new operational model in Sanyo now involved the potential for additional revenue. In addition to 12 months' salary, there were uncapped bonuses, based on strong employee performance. Importantly, financial incentives were developed based on a collaborative discussion of how to share bonuses. This provided a form of assurance to employees that adopting the RDHY principle was a positive step to take.

These actions by Haier were part of the strategy to address anxiety, a lack of trust and the uncertainty that usually accompanies mergers and acquisitions and to transform employee anxiety to a shared sense of ownership. Through a shared process of envisioning and uncovering individual visions (e.g. to be a global entrepreneur), an organisation is able to build intrapreneurs and leaders who will take pride in their work and in seeing their products sold in international markets. This approach demonstrates the important links between organisational values, communication, employee motivation and leadership. This is foundational to creating a conducive environment for building leadership in an interconnected ecosystem. As the ecosystem expands, this strategy for helping employees deal with organisational change offers value and is relevant for developing distributed forms of leadership within ecosystems. More and more, organisations have become diverse spaces in terms of social categories like race, gender, (dis)abilities and socioeconomic background. Also, the connected nature of the ecosystem redefines the boundaries of teams to include inter-organisational teams. A matrix organisational structure lends itself to the RDHY approach by dispensing with the traditional, narrow view of teams. With the rapid developments in technology, workspaces have also taken on a hybrid form where the notion of the organisation is both material and virtual; collaboration can be done face to face, virtually or via a combination of these. This postmodern view of what constitutes organisational boundaries, structure and spaces is integral to leading in an interconnected ecosystem, as the core strategy is underpinned by a win–win perspective which serves the common good.

Be a resilient leader

Resilience can be understood as the capacity of a thing to spring back from a difficult situation or adverse circumstances, or to recover and regain its original shape. It speaks of the ability to withstand challenges and maintain strength. In other words, it is a stress test. In relation to the organisation, we can also talk of resilience in relation to an individual (i.e. a leader or an employee), a team, an organisation and in technological terms. When we speak of resilience in relation to an individual, it is the ability to carry on being productive despite experiencing adverse situations. For a leader to be described as resilient, they must have attributes that enable them to bounce back into shape following a challenge that is often out of their comfort zone. Many circumstances present challenges for leaders and require the ability to adapt.

In contemporary organisations, the world of work has been characterised as comprising uncertainty, volatility, ambiguity and complexity, which means that leaders will often not have the luxury of remaining in comfort zones for extended periods. Resilience is therefore a key attribute for weathering the storms in difficult contexts, as Rotman professor Sarah Kaplan confirms in her study 'Why social responsibility produces more resilient organizations'.[6] Indeed, research shows that leaders are needed for creating or stabilising new organisations and for transforming failing ones. Both contexts present opportunities for demonstrating resilience as challenges are dealt with, managed or resolved. The 'great man' theory of leadership identifies key attributes of leaders such as the ability to inspire, communicate effectively and facilitate commitment to the achievement of a shared goal.

For an interconnected ecosystem, other leadership attributes are important, such as flexibility, ability to foster inclusion and cohesion amongst diverse groups and organisations, as well as sustaining collaborative relationships with them, the ability to identify potential collaborations and to expand the ecosystem meaningfully. This latter group of attributes deviates from the essentialist or static focus of the trait approach and recognises the need for adaptive capabilities of leaders. Leadership scholar Keith Grint[7] suggests a leadership approach that recognises that leadership traits are not static but can change over time, that environments and situations also change and that leaders have a key role in ensuring a form of stability that allows organisational stakeholders to continue to be productive. In this way, we can connect resilience in leadership to organisational resilience. This type of leadership can be summed up as entrepreneurial leadership, adding a new, entrepreneurial dimension to our understanding of leadership.

Jeffrey Timmons, in his book *The Entrepreneurial Mind*, described entrepreneurship as the ability to sense opportunities where others see chaos, to build something from practically nothing or a willingness to take calculated risks. Similarly, in a 2017 *Harvard Business Review* article,[8] entitled 'Hiring an entrepreneurial leader', Timothy Butler identified three key characteristics of entrepreneurs: the ability to thrive in uncertainty, a passionate desire to author and own projects, and a unique skill at persuasion. These traits enable a leader to be resilient – to make sense of changing contexts and also engage in sense-giving to employees, additionally helping them to understand the nuances involved and the implications for their productivity as well as meeting organisational goals. A deep understanding of customer needs, as argued in earlier sections, will enable a leader to sustain connections with customers and maintain connectivity across all three – the organisation, employees and customers.

Your company's financial performance matters

Resilience is only part of the journey towards performance in an ecosystem; measuring performance is an important way to assess if your actions and inputs translate into the desired output. There are different perspectives on what constitutes performance for an organisation, ranging from those emphasising quantitative indices to those emphasising qualitative indices. In conventional terms, performance involves an improvement over a previous state. In other words, growth and development can be seen as expressions of performance. Growth can be understood along different dimensions such as financial, knowledge, geographic, market share, customer base, company size, staff strength and partnerships. This means that you can pursue performance on multiple fronts. In addition to these dimensions, more recent attention has turned to other dimensions of performance, and these can be understood through the ESG framework, which refers to environmental, social and governance dimensions (see Kaplan and McMillan's 2021 study[9] as an example). Improvements along these dimensions can also be considered as growth. Aside from financial metrics, you should be able to articulate your purpose to speak to ESG concerns as more and more consumers are becoming selective about companies they work or do business with, as also argued in a 2021 study by Tomlinson et al.[10]

Some environmental changes have to do with effects of the organisation's direct activities on the environment in terms of pollution and depletion of natural resources. Other adverse changes in the environment may be caused by the supply chain. Companies are now giving more thought to where their raw materials are sourced and the consequent environmental impact. Against the backdrop of such changes, it is imperative that you are much more intentional about connecting with your discerning customers and leveraging the power of technology, digitisation and data analytics in doing so.

Additionally, globalisation and the rise of technology-enabled commerce mean that you also need to have a global focus, paying attention to the management of production facilities to meet global demand, and sustaining adequate inventory levels to support your product development and new product introduction. You will also need to be more aware of the scope of responsibility when it comes to sustainability issues. While your core production activities may not contribute directly to environmental degradation, the actions of other ecosystem members may do so. An integrated approach to ownership and responsibility means that you are actively involved in efforts and activities which address these environmental and social concerns. Irrespective of your level as a leader in your organisation, you need to hold yourself accountable. Governance is an area that signals to customers and employees that your organisation has their interests at heart. While leadership may be diffused in an ecosystem approach, it does not preclude having clear governance structures. In fact, good governance frameworks reinforce the centrality of the three key actors in the RDHY triad and their interconnectedness.

Paying attention to these dimensions of performance helps to ensure that you have a holistic view of the organisation and are adequately prepared to serve customers and employees towards realising organisational financial goals. This holistic stakeholder perspective requires you to demonstrate concern for people as well as the environment. It is, in fact, a means to ensuring sustainability of your enterprise within a wider, global ecosystem of people and nature. It allows your organisation to generate financial returns while remaining a responsible custodian of the social and physical environment. Haier's success within the energy-saving products space in its Internet of Air ecosystem, for instance, is an example of how innovation and financial performance can be integrated with ESG concerns. It allows EMCs to serve the customer's needs in an environmentally friendly way while also providing opportunities for employees to grow as individuals as they take on new leadership roles in driving EMCs.

Contrasting the two forms of leadership

As we have discussed so far, the practice of leadership within an organisation can take various forms. It must therefore be managed with intentionality in a way that generates the desired outcomes. Within the context of RDHY, two main forms of leadership emerge, as we have argued, the first being servant leadership and the other being leadership that operates within an interconnected organisation. Although both forms of leadership augur well for building organisational resilience and driving financial performance, managers must be conscientious in how they deploy leadership within their various organisations. In fact, apologists for any form of leadership (including dictatorial forms of leadership) can make this claim for their particular kind of leadership improving organisational performance. However, the proof is in the pudding. We have seen in our research of RDHY-practising organisations how leadership plays a role and the kind that makes an impact. It is leadership that serves – period. The goal is to know who is to be served and how to go about it.

In the case of servant leadership, the attention is often on the employee. This view also considers the employee as the one being led by another, the servant leader. As we demonstrated earlier, servant leadership has its challenges despite the many advantages it offers. The attention on the employee alone in this kind of leadership presents a narrow view of who is to be served. The converse is that attention is also on the leader who must develop certain traits that allow them to exhibit or demonstrate servanthood within the organisation. In both instances, several other factors, stakeholders, contexts and even non-humans such as technology are ignored. After all, the servant leader is there to serve the employee just as we see in Hesse's league of pilgrims where Leo is there to serve his team. This focus on the leader–employee relationship alone fails to recognise the bigger picture of the ecosystem within which the organisation operates. Additionally, a 'servant leader' assumes a 'king follower'. While this notion satisfies follower-centric leadership models, it distorts what leadership is really about. It should not be one party versus another, say, a leader versus a follower or a servant versus a king. Leadership is about influence, and it should not matter where that influence emerges from. In our view, servant leadership should be promoted in mentoring relationships where reverse mentoring is also possible. In this way, both mentor and mentee serve each other within the dyad and are able to satisfy each other's needs. In an organisational context where there are various stakeholders at play, servant leadership would work when it is deployed with other forms of leadership. It is in this light that we challenge managers to move beyond this form of leadership and embrace a much more complex view of their managerial contexts.

In the case of leadership that operates within an interconnected organisation, the picture is quite different. We choose not to label this kind of leadership, although we are tempted to call it service leadership as opposed to servant leadership in order to broaden its purpose. Labelling leadership is often unhelpful although it may provide some conceptual clarity. Our aim is not to promote a new leadership style but to show how managers can take advantage of the opportunities afforded by the Eastern philosophy of RDHY for management and to show its practical operability within organisations. Accordingly, it is better that we consider how this kind of leadership works for successful management of the organisation and what practical steps can be taken, rather than simply slapping a label on it. Now, whereas servant leadership serves the employee and simultaneously encourages the leader to develop 'servant traits', the kind of leadership we advocate serves all stakeholders within the ecosystem of the organisation.

Contrasting these two forms of leadership allows managers to see what areas of their current leadership practice can be improved to achieve this latter form of leadership that we advocate. By leadership in an interconnected ecosystem, we mean elevating what was ignored before, making visible what was off the radar before, and taking cognisance of what was taken for granted before. This means that even the very technologies within the organisation must no longer be taken for granted, and nor must the brick-and-mortar office spaces. In other words, this form of leadership is intentional about its decisions, actions and inactions within the organisation, but also 'outside' of it. We use the word 'outside' of the organisation cautiously as, in an interconnected organisation, the boundary between what is inside and what is outside is not so clear-cut and leaders must acknowledge this.

An ecosystem thinking jettisons insider–outsider dichotomies and embraces the wholeness of the organisation as an organism in its natural habitat whose spatial boundaries are undefined. If there is anything we have learnt within the last few decades of globalisation, it is that what affects one country is almost invariably bound to impact another, even if that other country is geo-politically different. Similarly, organisations are not closed off in silos but operate within their ecosystems whether they are aware of it or not. It takes the form of leadership that understands this interconnectedness to serve all stakeholders within the ecosystem. This leadership serves the employee, the customer, the organisation, various other partners it works with, and so on. To serve is to ensure there are enabling conditions while removing all kinds of constraints in the organisational environment. Customers must believe their voice is being heard, employees must feel appreciated and empowered to make decisions, and the organisation must look and feel humanised.

To deploy this leadership in an interconnected organisation, traits may be important but behaviour is more so. It is okay to allow people to come forward to take up leadership roles or drive new micro-communities within the organisation's ecosystem. They may feel the 'urge' to do so or may be recommended by their colleagues; more importantly, the behaviour of this kind of leadership is one that is in constant conversation with people within the organisation to build other leaders. This is the leadership that sustains resilience and drives financial performance.

Creating a roadmap for leadership development

Research has shown that an essentialist approach to leadership is outdated, and one cannot conclude that leaders are born with a set of finite traits or attributes. Rather, people can learn to be leaders, leaders can change over time and situations also constantly evolve. As a result, no matter where you are on your leadership journey, you can create a pathway for your development. The first step is to begin from where you are. It may be helpful to think about your previous experiences in leadership and even those actions you may regard as mistakes. When viewed through the lens of a student who is willing to learn, they represent opportunities for learning. Analyse what worked and what went wrong as well as what you could have done differently.

The second step is to look within yourself and identify any leadership gaps. By this, we mean developmental gaps that you may have in terms of the required leadership attributes. In particular, consider leadership traits that are needed for a dynamic and technology-driven world of work. More specifically, consider your approach to performance in all its dimensions, including financial and non-financial aspects and the ESG framework. Understand the different ways of viewing performance and what the implications are for the type of leader you need to be, in order to allow for flourishing on all fronts in your organisation and in the wider ecosystem. If there are areas where you need to build up on your knowledge and skills, identify formal and informal avenues to acquire this knowledge and skills. It could be through enrolling on a leadership course or programme, subscribing to practitioner journals for organisational leaders or having mentoring arrangements with more experienced leaders.

The third step is to build a compelling vision of what you aim to do in your future leadership practice. Make these stretch goals and work systematically towards achieving them. It may require you to be intentional about seeking opportunities to develop your leadership attributes and skills. Map out action plans that provide these opportunities and work towards them. You can also leverage the power of role models to help you develop future goals as you learn from their experiences. Role models can help to fast-track learning by presenting you with tailored content and giving you comments as feedback and feed-forward. In other words, through feedback, you learn about your past performance, while through feed-forward you proactively apply your new learning to future actions. Role models also serve as a source of accountability for leaders. As argued earlier, accountability is one way to communicate authenticity to a range of stakeholders. In leadership, it is beneficial to be accountable to the self, to mentors, employees, customers and other stakeholders. It communicates that a leader is open to learning and is cognisant of the trust invested in him or her by stakeholders. Accountability protects the leader from hubris, which, as a recent study by Laker et al.[11] highlights, leads to a slippery slope of leadership. Lastly, a leader needs to have a strong commitment to continuous learning and growth. This commitment ensures that whatever the situation may be, and whatever the challenges that emerge, the attitude is that of openness to learning, flexibility and a keen awareness of opportunities presented by dynamic work and business operating environments.

Chapter summary, reflective questions and practical implications

This chapter has focused on what it means to look beyond the conventional notion of servant leadership and to consider leadership that is relevant for a connected ecosystem. The context of a connected ecosystem requires leadership that is responsive, accountable and has a multi-perspective approach to relating with key actors in the ecosystem. To conclude this chapter, here are some reflective questions and top tips for personal development and professional development:

- *How would you appraise your personal leadership style?* One of the most uncomfortable exercises to engage in is an honest self-appraisal. However, to grow in leadership, an assessment of where you are and where you need to be is necessary. Identify your key strengths but also your weaknesses. You can personally draw up a list of your attributes and categorise them into strengths and weaknesses. You can also seek feedback from a range of others such as subordinates, colleagues and mentors. Having this 360-degree view of yourself will give you a holistic picture of your leadership practice. You can also conduct the Johari window exercise (see Chapter 8 for a description).

- *Thinking back, can you identify instances where you could have approached your own leadership practice a little differently?* It is important to recognise that no one knows it all and leadership can be learned. Assess your previous experience and face up to what you could have done differently. Keeping a reflective diary could help you to evaluate your own leadership but, more importantly, to revise the mental models you have used in the past. Peter Senge's old classic, *The Fifth Discipline*, published in 1990, still holds value for contemporary practice when it comes to how you might confront your own mental models.
- *What do your goals look like?* Move beyond the setting of SMART goals to setting FAST goals. Whereas SMART goals stand for those that are Specific, Measurable, Achievable, Relevant, and Time-bound, FAST goals are Frequently discussed, Ambitious, Specific (thus measurable) and Transparent. FAST goals allow you to engage with others more frequently to ensure shared ownership.
- *Could you approach someone more senior to be your mentor?* It is hugely beneficial to have a mentor as an accountability partner. You will learn from their experience, and they can be an invaluable source of ideas. They can also serve as a sounding board for your ideas.

References

1. Bennis, W. & Nanus, B. (2003) *Leaders: strategies for taking charge.* New York: HarperCollins Publishers.
2. Grint, K. (2005) *Leadership: limits and possibilities.* Basingstoke: Palgrave Macmillan.
3. Greenleaf, R. K. (1991) *Servant leadership: a journey into the nature of legitimate power and greatness.* New York: Paulist Press.
4. Fiedler, F. (1967) *A theory of leadership effectiveness.* New York: McGraw-Hill.

5. Tanenbaum, R. & Schmidt, W. H. (1973) 'How to choose a leadership pattern', *Harvard Business Review*, available at https://hbr.org/1973/05/how-to-choose-a-leadership-pattern (accessed 15 November 2022).
6. Kaplan, S. (2020) 'Why social responsibility produces more resilient organizations', *MIT Sloan Management Review*, available at https://sloanreview.mit.edu/article/why-social-responsibility-produces-more-resilient-organizations/ (accessed 15 November 2022).
7. Grint, K. (2000) *The arts of leadership*. Oxford University Press.
8. Butler T. (2017) 'Hiring the entrepreneurial leader', *Harvard Business Review*, available at https://hbr.org/2017/03/hiring-an-entrepreneurial-leader (accessed 19 August 2022).
9. Kaplan, R. S. & McMillan, D. (2021) 'Reimagining the balanced scorecard for the ESG era', *Harvard Business Review*, available at https://hbr.org/2021/02/reimagining-the-balanced-scorecard-for-the-esg-era (accessed 15 November 2022).
10. Tomlinson, B., Whelan, T. & Eckerle, K. (2021). 'How to bring ESG into the quarterly earnings call', *MIT Sloan Management Review*, available at https://sloanreview.mit.edu/article/how-to-bring-esg-into-the-quarterly-earnings-call/ (accessed 15 November 2022).
11. Laker, B., Cobb, D & Trehan, R (2021) *Too proud to lead: how hubris can destroy effective leadership and What to do about it*. Bloomsbury Business.

Bibliography

Hesse, H. (2013) *The journey to the east*. Important Books.

Sinek, S. (2017) *Leaders eat last: why some teams pull together and others don't*, 1st edition. Penguin.

Sull, D. & Sull, C. (2018) 'With goals, FAST beats SMART', *MIT Sloan Management Review*, available at https://sloanreview.mit.edu/article/with-goals-fast-beats-smart/ (accessed 15 November 2022).

Timmons, J. A. (1989) *The entrepreneurial mindset*. Brick House Pub Co.

Mark the trajectory

Introduction

The adoption of any management principle must be done with intentionality and careful planning. This must often be accompanied by a process of monitoring and evaluation in order to measure success or failure. Whereas the concepts of success and failure are often subjective and elusive in meaning, we can minimise the blurred lines between them and measure what is 'successful' or 'failed'. This can be done through the laying out of some 'objective' measures with which to benchmark your performance as a leader. We place 'objective' in inverted commas here to denote care in its usage, and you should too. This is because in marking the trajectory of your business as you deploy the principles of RenDanHeYi (RDHY), your own leadership journey, and the uptake of a new organisational culture that RDHY imposes, you might want to consider your own unique context and design the needed monitoring measures. This is often a subjective thing to do and there is nothing wrong with it. What matters is that you do this in a sensible and defensible way as you mark the trajectory, which is aptly the title of this penultimate chapter. We will examine how you can practically adopt and measure the RDHY model for your own business. You can then share your transformational story, which helps to embed your success even more.

Understand your context

Why is it important to understand your context? In this book, you have learnt much about Haier and other organisations. You have seen how they have applied the RDHY principles to grow their business and expand their ecosystems. But these contexts may be different from yours, you might say, and you would be right. Indeed, underpinning the success of RDHY is a deep understanding of the players in that specific context. You may be reading this book from a different part of the world where business is conducted differently and work cultures are different. While the Chinese context is known to be a collectivist one, we also know that there are strong elements of command-and-control type structures reinforced by power distance. Power distance refers to acceptance of hierarchy and inequality in a society. All of these features combine to give the context within which Haier built its ecosystem with a unique identity. By drawing on a deep understanding of this context, Zhang Ruimin was able to bring about transformation in his organisation.

But in your case, you may be in a context with a different set of factors at play. You might be operating in what is known as an individualistic environment, where despite the existence of teams, there is a strong drive by individuals to pursue their personal goals rather than have a collective outlook, and reward systems are designed to encourage such behaviours. The structure of your own organisation may also be hierarchical and bureaucratic, and indeed, changing this structure is hard work because people find it easier to remain in their comfort zones. The key point is for you, like Ruimin, to translate your deep understanding of your own context into solutions that will bring about the needed change. In other words, change brought about by an RDHY-driven shift from a bounded organisation to having open boundaries, from hierarchical structures to flatter structures, from competition to collaboration and from centralised leadership to shared power and service leadership.

Understanding your context also means recognising its strengths, opportunities, weaknesses and threats. Strengths might include a mature technology environment which allows for collaboration and efficient communication with users and employees alike, but which has not been explored due to an inward organisational focus within a closed boundary. A strength may also be a friendly legal environment for business which encourages investments in specific geographical areas or industries. Have you explored these? There may be tax advantages attached to these. All of this helps to inform your understanding of what your own context offers you and how you may take advantage of the available opportunities. Knowing where you are helps you to map where you want to go and your route there. So, these strengths may house opportunities as yet untapped, and it is your task to seek them out.

How about weaknesses in your context? You need to consider these as well and have an objective assessment of factors that may inhibit or limit your ability to benefit fully from an RDHY approach. They may have to do with your preconceived notions about how business ought to work, inherent biases or your limited access to knowledge or information. This can be a major stumbling block, as change in this case starts from the leader. Overcoming this barrier means that you are open to trying out new ideas, particularly when they are evidence-based. Your flexibility in this regard is worth emphasising, as it will have a positive knock-on effect on the rest of your organisation. When your employees see a shift in your disposition to the 'new', they will be encouraged to do the same. This is particularly important when you are facing cultural barriers to change, which are often difficult to overcome, as ways of doing things and the reasons for doing so have become so entrenched that people would rather play it safe than try something new. So, consider what weaknesses exist in your context as well as what stands as threats to the success of your journey to your ecosystem. Your strengths can signal to you where opportunities may lie, while your weaknesses may indicate areas that need strengthening. Sometimes you may discover blind spots that need addressing. We will say more on your personal leadership in the next section, but for now, think broadly about the unique features of your own context and what you can do about them.

When we talk about ecosystems, we are naturally talking about a network of partners and collaborators joined by common interests. Part of understanding your context is finding out who your potential collaborators could be. What organisations and businesses can you work with to create new value for your users? This may require you to take some time to think outside the box and broaden your horizon. Potential collaborators may be in the areas of research and development, idea generation, delivery of services to users or mechanisms for feedback generation. Take a closer look at organisations that you may previously have thought were firmly outside your industry; they may not be as distant as you previously thought.

In an ecosystem era, technology is key to connectivity – connecting organisations with one another, organisations with their employees, and employees with users. In understanding your own context, consider how developed your technology environment is. You also need to (re)examine your technology needs and figure out what you need technology to do for you. Investing in technology is a strategic decision with a long-term perspective. So, your choice must align with your value proposition. Once you have this clearly spelt out, then you can begin to consider the different options available. Expats and consultants can be useful in giving you an idea of a range of technology solutions. However, your decision would be based on your assessment of the costs versus the benefits. Also think about a back-up plan, should the technology run into difficulty. This would enable you to stay in business despite temporary glitches. So, understanding your context is a necessary first step in moving to an ecosystem approach to running your business. Let us now turn to your personal approach to leadership.

Analyse your own leadership

The concept of leadership has received a lot of attention over the years and we wonder why there continue to be books and articles written about it. The answer to this is simple. No matter how many materials there are about leadership, we cannot reduce it to something calculable or tangible to-dos. This is because leadership is a complex phenomenon and continues to be elusive in its definition. As management scholars, we have researched this concept from various perspectives and philosophical positions over several years and can tell you this one fact: *leadership has to do with three elements*. The three elements we posit have nothing to do with 'leaders' and 'followers' as several leadership materials would have us believe. You may have already noticed the critical stance we have taken in this book with regard to leadership as far as RDHY is concerned. For us, the reduction of a complex concept such as leadership to 'those who lead' and 'those who follow' does not offer any understanding of how managers in today's organisations must lead. From that view, let us now examine what those three elements of leadership are and then think about how you can analyse your own leadership as a manager in today's world of work.

Leadership is about the *personal*, the *communal* and the *contextual* range of factors that make up what it is in any given situation. These three elements have run through all theories of leadership over the last century and remain so today. Let's take each of these to analyse and examine how you can practically situate your own practice within them. First, the personal. In this element of leadership, it is all about you, the individual manager. Take a pause and think about that. Yes, the personal element of leadership has to do with *you*. At this point you may be asking yourself why we seem to be conflating the words 'leader' and 'manager' when nearly every book tells us that leadership is not the same as management. It all sounds nice when these sorts of ideas appear in 140-character tweets or in social media posts with several thousands of 'likes'. Really? You wouldn't employ someone to be a leader of operations in your company and then employ another individual as a manager of operations, would you? Or perhaps advertise a job for store manager and another for store leader and have them play separate roles in your company, would you? You get the point. This idea of conceptually reducing 'managers' to a lower level while placing 'leaders' on a higher plane is akin to ignoring a thundering herd of elephants in the room, because we all know it is managers who do the work of leadership. Management expert Henry Mintzberg has a lot more to say about this and we will recommend his books if you want to pursue that argument a bit more. For now, let's return to what we mean by the personal element of leadership in your practice as a manager.

It is in the space of the personal element of leadership that we think about individual traits and behaviours. In other words, you don't have to carry a title or hold a high position in your organisation to exercise the personal elements of leadership. Accordingly, every member of your organisation must exercise leadership. This is what the philosophy of RDHY underscores. It is a clarion call that no matter what position you hold in your organisation, you can rise to the challenge of leadership. You are a leader, and your employees are also all leaders. At the personal level, self-leadership becomes central in your practice. Those who cannot lead their own selves are simply not fit to lead. In self-leadership you acknowledge personhood, that is, your individuality, your strengths as well as your weaknesses, and being aware that your actions have a profound impact on those you work with in your organisation. This calls for being *reflective* and taking *reflexive* steps to correct your behaviour or actions. While *reflection* is about giving due consideration to previous experiences or actions and generating learning, *reflexivity* is more about taking immediate corrective actions in relation to what was reflected upon. These important skills of reflection and reflexivity seem missing in many leadership models but are central to self-leadership and being a reflective practitioner.

To analyse your own leadership as a manager, honesty is fundamental. This involves being honest with yourself and encouraging honesty in relation to you by others. One helpful tool you can use for this is the Johari window. The term 'Johari' is a mash-up of the first names of the scholars whose work it is based on. 'Jo' from Joseph Luft (1916–2014) and 'hari' from Harrington Ingham (1916–1995) who were eminent psychologists of the twentieth century who together and developed the Johari window in 1955. They call on individuals to reflect on what they know or don't know about themselves while inviting others to also indicate what they know or don't know about the individual in question. We present this more clearly in Figure 8.1.

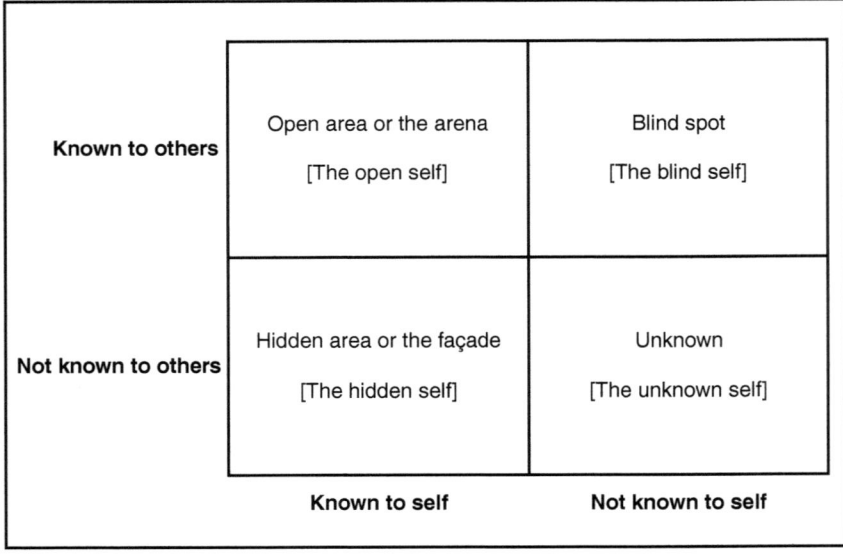

Figure 8.1 The Johari window developed by Luft and Ingham (1955).

As illustrated in the figure, the starting point in analysing your own self-leadership is a reflection on what you know as well as what others know about you. This brings us to the second element of leadership, which is the *communal*. You cannot analyse your own leadership without due consideration to the community of your practice. Nobody is a leader in a vacuum. Leadership is a concept that plays out in the community, be that only one other person or several other people. That community of your practice might include colleagues in the organisation, your managers, those who report to you, and your customers. In other words, you can obtain feedback from your community in some sort of 360-degree style as you fill out those aspects of the Johari window where their voice matters. While the Johari window was originally designed to be populated with a specific pool of words, we encourage you to be open-ended without being limited to specific vocabulary. In this way, you allow the voice of those assessing you to be as verbatim as possible.

Analysing your self-leadership with the Johari window reveals your 'four selves' – these are the open self, the hidden self, the blind self, and the unknown self. Your open self captures what you know about yourself as well as what others know about you. It is like playing in the open arena. For example, you know you are a meticulous individual and others know this about you. It is therefore no news to you if someone new interacts with you and tells you that you are a meticulous individual. However, that still matters, as it *confirms* to you what it is that you already know. The confirmation by others gives you an opportunity to build upon your leadership or lead with greater awareness and intentionality. This is because your leadership in the open self is what is out there for all to see. In other words, you are on the open stage where you are highly visible, you know what you're doing and are aware that other people in your community know what you are doing. Simply put, your leadership in the open self is where you confirm what you already know. Remember that the key is to be honest with yourself and to encourage honesty from those assessing your leadership. What this means is that your open self can also tell you what you might not want to hear although you know it is true. For instance, you would (hopefully) know if you're a difficult person to deal with and are aware that others know this about you, but you would rather not hear it in plain language. This is where honesty matters in this self-assessment. If your open self confirms that you are a terrible leader, you may be filled with hubris and your haughtiness will soon catch up with you if you don't change.

Conversely, your hidden self is that aspect of your self-leadership where only you know what you know about you – nobody else does. This may include your inner motivations, anxieties, worries, fears and the insecurities you have. Perhaps there are things you fear might be considered as weaknesses by others, if they knew. Whereas your hidden self may be a driving force in your leadership, e.g. your 'why', it can also be simply a façade or something detrimental to your leadership if it produces negative emotions inside you. On this latter point, it can kill you softly while you hold on to it. It doesn't have to be this way, as you can take steps to deal with your hidden self. To do so demands placing your trust in a select group of people that you can invite into that hidden space. After all, it may be that what you think is hidden from others is something they already know, in which case it would be helpful and developmental for you to let others into your not-so-hidden space.

The communal element of your leadership is pronounced in your blind self. This is in reference to those things that you have no clue about with regard to your leadership, only in this instance your community of practice is very much in the know. This is your blind spot. Others know stuff about your leadership, but you have no idea what those things are. This is an incredibly important factor in the analysis of your self-leadership. Knowing or reducing your blind spot can improve your self-awareness and overall leadership practice. It takes humility to accept your blind spots and not feel as though others are picking you apart. You can have conversations about your blind self with your trusted colleagues and work towards improving yourself as a leader in your ecosystem. Within a highly interconnected ecosystem, you don't want to be a leader who is unaware of what others already know. In fact, your organisation's future may be put at risk if your blind spots are so big that you even miss out on the ongoing trends (see Case Study 8.1 on Nokia's blind spot).

The final quadrant in the Johari window (see Figure 8.1) refers to your unknown self. This speaks to those factors about you that

Case Study 8.1

Nokia's blind spot

Nokia, incorporated in 1865, was a strong technology organisation until that story changed in the early 2000s. Nokia rose to become the world's most important, albeit short-lived, mobile phone manufacturing company. It was popular and almost difficult to see any other company taking Nokia's leading position in the market. Nokia phones were of high quality and their range of products were second to none in the mobile phone industry. However, at the turn of the millennium, Apple, Samsung and other smaller technology organisations entered the market with mobile devices and phones that provided touchscreen functionality. A new trend had begun, and everyone in the industry could see this new trend, but somehow, Nokia was blindsided by it. By the time Nokia got into making touchscreen phones, it was too late; the market had shifted. Ironically, Nokia had invented a touchscreen-capable and Internet-enabled mobile in its laboratories three years before Apple's iPhone was launched. Ari Hakkarainen, a Nokia employee in its marketing division, is quoted in *The New York Times* to have said, 'It was very early days, and no one really knew anything about the touchscreen's potential' and that 'management worried that the product could be a costly flop'. Well, it was indeed a costly flop, but it was a flop for the entire company not to pursue what they could have been leaders in. Touch-sensitive smartphones had taken over the market and Nokia simply could not see it until they lost their competitive position. It all happened in their blind spot. The company was eventually acquired by Microsoft in 2016. Nobody could explain what really happened to Nokia better than Stephen Elop, its CEO at the time of its acquisition. In Elop's emotive farewell speech at his final press conference after Nokia's acquisition, he concluded, 'We didn't do anything wrong, but somehow, we lost.' He and his management team then broke down in tears.

are unknown to you and also unknown to others. These are your 'unknown unknowns' and are out there for you to discover as you seek continuous growth. However, we suggest that if some aspects of your leadership are unknown to others and are unknown to you, there is no need to spend your energy on them. It is an exercise in futility to want to correct or develop what you don't know. It is your blind spot you should be worried about as it can render your leadership ineffective. As we have established earlier in this book, you want to grow your business with ecosystem thinking and that requires a greater sense of awareness of your business environment and you should therefore seek to reduce your blind spot. Again, you can do this by engaging your community in an honest way. In other words, you should boldly activate the communal element of your leadership for your advantage as you analyse your self-leadership and develop yourself within the ecosystem. You can only do this by jettisoning the irredeemably hopeless idea of 'leaders and followers', as we have argued earlier. If people are only 'following' you, how would you know what they've got to say to help you discover your blind self? Metaphorically, you would have to stop walking or running until all your 'followers' caught up with you and then let you know what you couldn't see behind you. You get the point – it is simply untenable to position the concept of leadership in this way.

One practical way by which some organisations analyse self-leadership is the use of 360-degree feedback. This is not necessarily a bad strategy; however, it often puts the leader under the hand lens of public gaze with the leader facing the heat while everyone else is an anonymous spectator. Overall bad feedback would thus lead to paranoia, which does not augur well for leadership, which we have established is not only personal but communal. It is better to have meaningful conversations in your analysis of self-leadership than to hide behind anonymous surveys that 360-degree and other feedback mechanisms offer for leadership practice. It is often an emotional venture to invite others to take part in your analysis of self-leadership, particularly with the Johari window. It tells your community you are human. Your humanity is something to embrace, display and celebrate. RDHY is a human-centric philosophy that does not seek to make heroes and villains but to engage with one's humanity and limitless potential. The communal element of leadership is thus key to your personal leadership journey. You should use it. Management scholar Henry Mintzberg recognises this and argues, 'Enough leadership. Time for communityship'. In his view, leadership often invokes the image of a 'great white knight riding in on a great white horse to save us all (even if headed into a black hole).' We have already argued the hopeless nature of this argument and therefore need not belabour the point. Assessing your leadership through the lens of the personal and the communal is therefore key to developing you and your organisation under RDHY, which operates with an ecosystem thinking.

Earlier, we mentioned that the concept of leadership has three elements to it: the *personal*, the *communal* and the *contextual*. We have now detailed the first two, but we should highlight that the third element – the *contextual* – speaks to the array of interconnected materials, resources, factors, tangible and intangible assets, etc. that together make up the domain within which leadership is practised. Simply put, the *contextual* is about your ecosystem and this too must be analysed.

Analyse your ecosystem – map out the terrain

Let us now turn to the ecosystem within which you exist as an organisation. The well-known saying 'no man is an island' rings true here. As a business, you are not an island that operates on your own. You exist within a network of actors, i.e. your unique context. Whether you produce a physical good (product) or a service, certain inputs go into the production of your value for your customer. These inputs come from a range of resources, including labour, capital, land, raw materials and your entrepreneurial skills. Sometimes you utilise products that are produced by another company but which are intermediate goods that go into your own production process as inputs. Those who supply you with resources for producing value are a key part of your ecosystem. They are your suppliers and they often transcend geographical boundaries.

The users of your product are also part of your ecosystem as they depend on you to meet their needs. We have talked about users in earlier chapters and why they are central to your ecosystem. How can you know what your users or customers need today? Speak to them. You can run engagement sessions to keep abreast of how their needs are changing or where their tastes might be headed in the near future. In-person sessions are powerful for establishing trust because they offer opportunities for you to experience non-verbal cues that complement and reinforce communication between you and your customers. As mentioned before, you can invite your customers into your company for site visits (as Zhang Ruimin did) to give them a stronger sense of ownership. You can also complement these with online sessions for sharing ideas and brainstorming. In recent times where digital technologies abound, virtual site visits should be a no-brainer. This is even more important as your users will most likely extend beyond your national geographical boundaries.

We have established that your suppliers enable you to produce value for your users. However, your ecosystem is much broader than this linear view of suppliers–producer–users. You operate within a regulatory environment and therefore the regulatory authority, or government, is also an important player in your ecosystem. Government economic, fiscal or monetary policy can constrain or enable your business activities. Interest rates can affect your ability to access credit or financing for expanding your business just as a squeeze on disposable income as a result of increased taxes can affect the demand for your products. So, the decisions you make need to factor in the short-, medium- and long-term thinking of the government regarding your industry and, more broadly, economic development.

It would be simplistic to think that you are the only one interested in your line of business. Even if this is the case at present, it may not remain so for long. The point being made here is that you will always have competition – other organisations in your line of business who are also aiming to provide value to the customer. Remember, the customer can easily be distracted by the number of product offerings out there. This is the effect of competition in your space. To build a sustainable ecosystem, you need to start thinking differently about these competitors. Rather than the typical winner-takes-all mentality, start to think about a win–win strategy where everyone gives and receives value. Indeed, this is a very different way of thinking about those who are competing with you for market size, revenue and profits. However, we are talking about building an ecosystem given the opportunities that exist in your context. This requires thinking differently. In mapping out the terrain of your ecosystem, identify these key players and start to consider how you can work collaboratively with them to produce value.

There is an important group within your ecosystem that is often downplayed. You may have guessed it – they are your employees. Sometimes, strategic discussions about company growth often see employees as one of the factors of production that can be assumed to be a constant, in much the same way we assume that production equipment is a constant, rather than a variable. But we know now more than ever before that employees no longer stay with one organisation from their initial appointment until retirement. Labour has become mobile and many employees have become more demanding in terms of what they want out of work and their working. The popular expression – the great resignation – typifies this exodus of employees from organisations due to shifts in personal values, a desire for work–life balance and flexible working as well as working conditions that allow for flourishing. In building a sustainable ecosystem, therefore, employees cannot be viewed as a constant. To keep them, however, you as a leader must work on securing their buy-in to the new way of working – the RDHY approach and an ecosystem which continuously seeks to produce value for all. To bring them on board, you can have open and honest conversations with your employees about what is meaningful to them. This helps to build an atmosphere of trust and is the foundation for engaged and committed workers.

Analysing your ecosystem therefore demands that you know who the players in the ecosystem are. Identifying these players is the first step to building a strong ecosystem. You can then think about the various connections that must be established. Who in your ecosystem has the greatest influence with regard to your business outcomes? Who do you need to help you achieve your objectives? Who has the power to make it happen for you? When you analyse your ecosystem, you are able to see where the gaps are and what you need to do in order to strengthen your position, realign yourself or form new alliances within it.

Assessing, measuring and improving your performance

So, having analysed your context, examined your personal leadership style, signalled the new direction to your employees and customers, and begun to outline the scope of your ecosystem, what's next? It is to see how well you are doing on each front. It is important to track your progress (or lack of it) so as to undertake remedial action which ensures you are still on the road to achieving your goals. Even as you measure your performance in a certain time period, conditions surrounding your business may change and have an impact on your future performance. One thing that is certain is that nothing remains fixed for long. The world of work is a dynamic one and operating contexts are no different. The idea is that you need to continuously scan your environment and make adjustments where necessary. Many good ideas start well but lose steam after a while or completely fail. A common example is the failure rate of start-ups today – a whopping 50% fail within the first five years. To avoid this, it is vital to have a mechanism in place for retrieving and processing new information about your ecosystem and feeding this into your strategic decisions. We have talked about the players in your ecosystem and how you can begin to develop more meaningful relationships with them such that you jointly create value. Let's begin with the RDHY triad – your organisation, its employees and users. How can you measure how well the relationships are deepening and the outcome of such connections? At this point, we will consider the case of Haier and how the company went about measuring the deployment of RDHY within its ecosystem (see Case Study 8.2).

It is understandable that how you measure your own performance in your organisation will be different from what Haier does with its practice of RDHY. In the following, we outline a tool for you to adapt or modify to obtain a scorecard that measures your progress in building successful EMCs (see also Figure 8.2). We have used our learning of Haier's own scorecard to qualitatively develop this simplified tool for your consideration.

In the scorecard, you have a set of metrics that you can use to assess your organisation's readiness for implementing RDHY. For each of the dimensions for assessing your organisation's microenterprises,

> **Case Study 8.2**
>
> ## Haier and ecosystem micro-community performance measurement
>
> **Deepening the organisation–employee connection**
> In implementing RDHY, the first step Haier took in deepening its connection with its employees was to break down barriers constituted by a strongly hierarchical system. Haier let go of about 12,000 middle managers, giving these managers the option of either becoming 'entrepreneurs' within the company or leaving the organisation entirely. While a small group left the company, the majority opted to become the first entrepreneurs under the new RDHY system. Whereas the previous structure had emphasised superiority and rank, the new system signalled that each employee was an autonomous entrepreneur and therefore not subordinate to anyone. They now had the freedom to pursue their ideas and achieve personal fulfilment in the process. To support this new role, Haier delegated three powers to its now autonomous employees: the power to hire and fire, the power to make business decisions, and the power to share profits made from their economic activities. It was clear that the entrepreneurs could not act alone but needed to function in a small team of microenterprises composed of other entrepreneurs.
>
> So, Haier effectively empowered its autonomous employees to take the second step, which was to form these microenterprises. Each microenterprise worked towards a central goal, which was to create value for users and share profits realised in the process. Flexibility was a part of how the microenterprise worked, as the central goal was not always cast in stone. Through collaborative discussions, they were able to agree on new goals where needed and channel their efforts towards achieving these. In this case, they could also select another person to lead the microenterprise. These decisions were taken at the micro level and were not imposed on the unit by the Haier group or its executives. If, however, the project was much bigger than what the microenterprise

▶

could handle, several microenterprises came together to form a community – known as an ecosystem micro-community (EMC). This is the third step in the process of building an organisational ecosystem. The unmet needs of users represent the glue holding these EMCs together, as each unit works to meet some dimension of user needs. This structural change was geared at maximising the value of the individual and creating conditions that can help autonomous employees to do so. Whereas in traditional organisational settings, shareholder value takes primacy, driven by actions and evaluations of the executive team, under RDHY, employees create and maximise their individual value through the autonomy given to them. Employee value, underpinned by autonomy and an enduring sense of purpose, is also seen to contribute to shareholder value.

Direct engagement with users
Haier gauges the success of its EMCs by measuring not just value creation but also how many lifetime users it has generated. It recognises that this cannot be achieved by a single organisation, but by a dynamic network of actors in an ecosystem, creating personalised value for user needs. As such, it prioritises direct engagement with users and the aim is to organically connect users and the organisations in the ecosystem in such a way that there is co-evolution as they both respond to changes in the operating environment, particularly responding to changes in the needs of different user groups. A core feature of how Haier measures its success is found in the EMC contract with employees, where it tries to balance user experience with solutions created. Within the larger organisation there is a network of EMCs where some are responsible for delivering user experience as a value to the customer and others are tasked with delivering solutions based on the information gathered from user-experience EMCs. There is also an RDHY scorecard which the organisation uses to capture the evolution of the EMCs along two broad dimensions of self-sustenance as a micro-community, on the one hand, and customer value creation on the other.

Ecosystem positioning (measures the extent to which a microenterprise has engaged other actors within its ecosystem to achieve its aims)	Awareness of actors Score 1-5	Engagement with actors Score 1-5	Established collaboration Score 1-5	Total score for EMC positioning
Self-managed (measures the extent to which the microenterprise has managed its operations in delivering customer value)	Financial sustenance Score 1-5	Employee autonomy Score 1-5	Technology-driven operations Score 1-5	Total score for self-managing
Self-organised (measures the extent to which the microenterprise has recruited and/or retained talent and employee motivation)	Employee hiring Score 1-5	Employee retention Score 1-5	Employee motivation Score 1-5	Total score for self-organising

Figure 8.2 A simplified RDHY organisational assessment tool.

i.e. ecosystem positioning, self-management and self-organising, as illustrated in Figure 8.2, you may assign scores for individual components such as 1 = poor, 2 = fair, 3 = good, 4 = very good and 5 = excellent. Converting your qualitative assessment into quantitative measures would help you to monitor progress in snapshots for easy dissemination. In other words, you can evaluate the positioning of your microenterprises, how well they self-manage as well as dimensions of self-organisation. For larger organisations which themselves may constitute a community or an ecosystem of sorts, this tool is also useful for checking readiness for implementing RDHY. Figure 8.3 offers a way to qualitatively examine value creation in your organisation and provides dimensions that can be assessed, ranging from value proposition to delivery and

Proposed value (measures the desirability, feasibility and viability of the product or service)	Desirability Score 1–5	Feasibility Score 1–5	Viability Score 1–5	Total score for proposed value
Value delivered (measures the number and quality of products and services created for the customer)	Ideas generated Score 1–5	Quantity produced Score 1–5	Customer satisfaction Score 1–5	Total score for value delivered
Shared value (measures income generated and profit shared among all employees in the microenterprise with reference to the previous year)	Income generated Score 1–5	Profit shared Score 1–5	Ecosystem value Score 1–5	Total score for value shared

Figure 8.3 A simplified RDHY value matrix.

thereafter to value sharing. These dimensions give greater focus to your activities in terms of solutions that will satisfy user needs and are helpful for your process of re-evaluating your relationship with the various stakeholders within your ecosystem. You can develop each of the components into more detailed surveys, but the rating scale provided in Figure 8.3 offers a starting point that allows you to appraise how well your organisation or newly formed EMC is maturing, i.e. in terms of value creation. It is worth noting that this exercise is not a one-off but can be used at different points in time to check progress towards a more coherent and functional ecosystem.

Translating your learning from RenDanHeYi to your own context

There are several lessons to be taken away from the Haier EMC performance measurement model. What is clear is that the company's emphasis is on some key values such as autonomy, human dignity, flexibility, creativity, responsiveness to users and timeliness. In translating this learning to your own context, a good place to start is in the area of your core organisational values. This is not unconnected with what your values are as a leader. What is important is recognising where disparities may lie, as contemporary organisations are known to be sites of value diversity. Your role, as mentioned earlier, is to bring your employees with you on this journey of change. This collaborative approach is a useful way to demonstrate how your ecosystem will function based on open conversations and shared values.

The dignity of the human being premised upon autonomy is not an idea that is unique to the Orient; as far as human ethics are concerned, it is universal. As a result, it is possible to apply and adapt the principles of RDHY to different contexts. The aim of this book is not to prescribe an off-the-shelf solution that is cast in stone and ready for direct deployment but to stimulate you as a leader to be creative about how RDHY can work in your context. For this reason, we have identified the key values driving the actions of Haier in developing its own ecosystem. To begin with, you can work with the simplified scorecards provided in Figures 8.2 and 8.3 to get a sense of where you are as an organisation. But beyond this, look within your own organisation and try to articulate what your core values are. This is not an exercise that requires simply going to your organisation's website and taking the statements stated there. It is an honest look at what is truly valued – in practice. You may find that there is a gap between both. In this case, then your list of values must be the latter – what you can see in practice.

Next, try to compare these with the values embedded within RDHY practice. Do you find any similarities or is the gap even wider? This exercise is important for laying the foundation of what your new organisational structure would look like. Bear in mind that the aim is not to uncritically reproduce another Haier but to creatively develop an ecosystem model which works for you and delivers the intended benefits. The next thing to assess is your organisational structure. Consider what type of changes you can make in your structure that would allow you to express these new sets of values. You may think about a radical shift to a flatter structure or you can choose to maintain a matrix structure. In your decision-making, keep the values at the heart of the changes you intend to make.

Apply this same principle to the evaluation of your relationships with members of your ecosystem – suppliers, regulatory agencies, users, employees, etc. Similarly, think about how technology can be deployed to help you in achieving those goals you have set so that the new vision for your organisation materialises.

Assessing progress from one point to another necessitates comparing current performance with a baseline. For you, that baseline could be where you are now. It is important to articulate the different areas along which you will assess your progress. For example, you can consider removing layers of bureaucracy which are unnecessary. Examine your processes and see how you can streamline them such that, with fewer steps, the same result can be achieved. Technology can often be an aide, helping you to simplify your business processes. Decisions about which technology to adopt could also be opened up to a collaborative discussion among your employees, such that you create buy-in from the start. You can encourage the entrepreneurial spirit by running ideation sessions regularly, giving employees opportunities to come up with creative ideas that can expand your business. Keep track of these ideas and how they are gradually translated into innovation for your business, with your employees taking the lead. Responsibility, flexibility and autonomy can be incredibly motivating for employees who have been used to a previous era of command and control. How about the way you reward your employees? This may require revising your reward systems such that it motivates employees to channel their energies into generating creative ideas which are profitable and also meet customer needs. Performance-related pay systems have been used for years and offer value for opening up additional earning potential for employees. Now, you might argue that such an extrinsic reward can crowd out intrinsic motivation. However, to counter this, like Haier, give the employee a stake in the business, if possible. Having a sense of ownership changes an employee from merely complying with rules to becoming a committed partner in the organisation.

How can you check that your employees are happy with the new direction? You can design feedback mechanisms to capture their reactions to how the new approach is working. As emphasised earlier, open and continuous communication with your stakeholders is key to sustaining engagement. Where you observe that progress is slow or lacking, you can collaboratively find ways to address the impediments by keeping communication lines open with your employees, customers, suppliers and ecosystem partners. Sometimes, the solution to challenges may be to allow a new idea to run as a separate entity – a subsidiary, a spin-off or even divestment. Making these changes moves you along your growth path as an organisation towards the stage where you begin to thrive within your ecosystem. One way to carry along your key stakeholders is to share stories of success and progress. When a new idea has been developed and becomes commercially successful, it is helpful to celebrate this by sharing the story with other units in your organisation. The intention is not just to motivate others to be entrepreneurial in their actions but also to build a cohesive ecosystem. In addition, hearing about progress in an area can inspire a creative spark in others which begins the formation of a new or related idea. Within your context, consider how you can best share stories of progress using in-person sessions or by leveraging technology. Sharing stories thus becomes a strategic tool to recognise the efforts of employees and customers, but also to motivate others to pursue their creative ideas as well. Sharing is central to the RDHY culture, as EMCs continuously exchange information that can provide value to users. This is not to say that there is a complete absence of competition in the ecosystem, but it has been greatly minimised because all participants are focused on value creation, knowing that they will, in turn, share out of the value.

Chapter summary, reflective questions and practical implications

This chapter has dealt with practical issues surrounding the implementation of RDHY and what that might mean for your context. It may seem a daunting task to start the process of changing from your familiar comfort zone to a new way of thinking about how your organisation is designed and your relationship with your employees, customers and even competitors. That is to be expected. However, you will never know what is on the other side if you remain where you are. And if there is one thing you can be certain of, it is that whether you do something about it or not, your playing field will continue to change. RDHY is already making a difference in several markets and the pace of innovation is relentless. Your response to this dynamic world will determine whether you will be a part of this wave or be swept away by it. There are examples of success stories to draw from as ideas about RDHY are gradually making their way into the world of work and more companies are realising the latent potential waiting to be unleashed. Let's tie up the essence of this chapter by offering you some specific questions to consider helping you make the shift:

- *How can you restructure your organisation such that it exemplifies your core values?* In restructuring your organisation, think about the ways you can expand the scope of your employees' roles so that they are empowered to take decisions and be autonomous. This way, you would be able to flatten your organisational hierarchy and set the stage for stronger collaboration among your employees.
- *How can you leverage technology to deepen your organisation–employee connection?* Think also about how you can move your employees and your organisation from indirect to direct engagement with users. Pay attention to how you would capture employee satisfaction with your EMC. You can utilise technology to help you in these areas by running instant polls instead of 15- to 20-minute surveys. Additionally, you could run a Johari window analysis for yourself and your managerial staff to obtain a bigger picture of your combined strengths and areas that may need to be worked on.
- *Who are the actors in your ecosystem?* We have emphasised the importance of deepening connections across the ecosystem as the hallmark of the RDHY approach. Consider how you can be creative in engaging collaboratively with your various stakeholders. As you engage with them, also put in place feedback mechanisms to capture your performance along specific indices that you have identified. All the lessons learnt in this book coalesce here for you. It is time to make that change.

Bibliography

Luft, J. & Ingham, H. (1955) 'The Johari window, a graphic model of interpersonal awareness', *Proceedings of the Western Training*

Laboratory in Group Development. Los Angeles: University of California, Los Angeles.

O'Brien, K. J. (2010) 'Nokia's new chief faces culture of complacency', *New York Times,* available at https://www.nytimes.com/2010/09/27/technology/27nokia.html (accessed 26 August 2022).

Stringer, C., Didham, J. & Theivananthampillai, P. (2011), 'Motivation, pay satisfaction, and job satisfaction of front-line employees', *Qualitative Research in Accounting & Management,* 8(2): 161–179.

Concluding thoughts

The writing of this book took us on a journey. As indicated at the start, we are management scholars trained in the West, with a Western worldview and various philosophical approaches that originate from Western thinking. In researching the ideas captured in this book, we have had to go through a paradigm shift by embracing an Eastern worldview. It is not as though one is better than the other, but that in seeing through the lens of others, we discover a new sense of reality. Additionally, we recognise the importance of context so that in your discovery, you consider how your own context can imbibe what it is that you have learnt from elsewhere.

Our first challenge, we believe yours also, was in how we could pronounce this Chinese word, RenDanHeYi. Although we have researched it, read broadly about it, interviewed its practitioners, and so on, we still pronounce it wrongly and that is okay. If you find it tongue-twisting to pronounce Ren-Dan-Her-Yee together in one go, you are not alone. You are still on that journey, as are we. The principles RDHY stands for, however, do not give us any pronunciation difficulty, which means we can take what matters and be the change that RDHY represents. Hopefully, this book has also taken you on that journey of discovery – a new way of seeing your organisation in relation to other now-significant players.

We began by setting the scene and acquainting you with how people have been organised in productive relations through time. We considered the key structural features in the first, second, third and fourth industrial revolutions and showed the limitations of these for organisational growth. In the second chapter, we zoomed in to the world of Haier, to show how its turnaround came about as a result of one man having the courage to disrupt the status quo, i.e. Zhang Ruimin, who embodied this idea of RDHY in his own practice as a leader. We unpacked what RDHY means in the succeeding chapters, first by showing the three key actors within the RDHY triad and the values underpinning the relations between them. We delved further to address each actor in turn, contrasting conventional ways of viewing the organisation, employees and customers with the new approach which seeks to close the distances we identified. We also explored your personal leadership practice and how the change must begin with you as the leader and how your understanding of leadership will evolve as you embrace a new paradigm.

We urge you to lead with RDHY and think about serving more than just the customer. The last chapter brings it all into perspective by offering you a way to harness the benefits of this new approach towards integrating the organisation, employees and users such that you build a sustainable ecosystem. We offer you a way to assess where you are at the moment and chart where you want to be. The scorecard we developed was adapted from the core principles underpinning RDHY to produce a simplified matrix of metrics that you could use. As we highlighted earlier, we strongly urge you to understand your context as this knowledge is foundational for bringing in the benefits of RDHY into your own space. With the several examples used throughout the book, we hope you have taken on board how RDHY has been implemented and, more importantly, why. For those organisations that have adopted RDHY, the results speak for themselves, and you too can be among them.

You may ask, 'Why is all this relevant to me at this time?'. As we established from the start, the world is constantly evolving. The move from one industrial revolution to another is evidence that such changes are global and have far-reaching effects. You are in the current epoch, with all its complexities and uncertainties, and the tide is high. Technology is developing at an unprecedented pace and disrupting established models of organisation. Today, a newly incorporated company can be born global and begin to compete with well-known brands. Wealth can be transferred from one part of the globe to another in the space of seconds or minutes. Indeed, as we identified, the world we operate in is volatile, uncertain, complex and ambiguous. And so, the survival of your organisation depends on how you navigate the complexities of this era. While you may not have control over external conditions, you can begin to shape them as you make a change, first in yourself and then in your organisation. The value is really in the willingness to take on this new lens and see with new eyes. In doing this, you will be able to spot opportunities where you had not seen them before.

We acknowledge that organisations are sites of diversity. This is even more so in this era where labour is mobile, and employees can easily move from one employer to another. Many organisations like yours have a multinational employee base and therefore you can expect that there are different values and ways of valuing. The challenge for you, therefore, is to get your people on board. As with any new initiative, there is a need to share the vision of the new direction of travel and secure buy-in. Leadership scholar Gary Yukl defines leadership as your ability to influence people in a specific direction. Importantly, it is being able to get them to agree on what needs to be done and how to do it, and harnessing individual and collective efforts towards the achievement of the goal. In this instance, it is no different. The task is to get not just employees this time, but also your stakeholders to understand this new way of working. It does not presuppose the complete absence of competition, as businesses will still operate based on their competitive advantages (remember your analysis of your strengths, weaknesses, opportunities and threats?). The new message you are getting across is that of a collaborative effort towards satisfying an ever-growing customer base and an ever-widening or evolving array of customer needs.

To effectively meet up with these challenges, a different approach to structuring the organisation and thinking about your organisation is needed. The ecosystem approach allows you to be responsive to your customers, who, as we have argued, are no longer outside the organisation in the traditional sense but are now co-creators of value. Your next step therefore is to begin to identify the players in your ecosystem and engage with them. As with many aspects of organisational life, this cannot be done on your own. Engaging your employees by empowering them will soon start to yield the results of commitment, creativity and productivity that you desire. Open communication and embracing feedback are your tools in this regard, as they will help you share the new philosophy but also give opportunity for others to make sense of it and come on board. There may be that odd person who takes a bit longer to get on the train, and that is to be expected. This is where sharing stories of progress becomes important. It will show clearly that the change is possible but also that the benefits are tangible.

Another thing to consider in understanding your own context is the diversity not just in terms of players but also in terms of values. Perhaps your industry has a unique set of values, some of which are core to your operations. Use the scorecard we provided as a starting point (see Chapter 8). But in re-envisioning where you want to be in the new ecosystem, identify your core values and this includes those that are fundamental to your industry. Articulate them as clear goals in your modified framework for performance evaluation and start to track your progress towards achieving them.

One question that may linger on your mind has to do with your competitors. You may say, 'I have looked at my ecosystem. In an era of branding, rivalry and rankings, there is still a lot of competition. How can I sell a win–win approach?'. This is a valid question to ask. However, the answer lies in the evidence. Today, Haier's success is recognised by organisations in the West, including well-known research and educational institutions such as Massachusetts Institute of Technology. The deployment of RDHY for transforming GE Appliances and its current operational structure in the white goods business has produced unprecedented outcomes. Results always speak for themselves. It might also be a good idea to see what is happening around you. Read about the Internet of Things and how Haier has revolutionised its approach to ecosystems such that you now have the Internet of Air, the Internet of Water, the Internet of Food, and so on. What does this mean? Haier is driving its own growth intentionally with ecosystems thinking, which brings together all players providing value at different points and in different ways. There is much to learn, and we hope this book offers you some starting points for your own journey.

Finally, if there's any true learning that we wish to establish from our research into RDHY, it is the need to be human-centric in our leadership practices. As we reflect on this, it is clear to us why this is crucial for our contemporary management practices where the focus has often been on various performance indices that point to the bottom line. Is this a bad thing? Well, although it is not a bad thing to make profit, what RDHY really challenges you to think about is whether profit is really your *why* of being in business. In

CONCLUDING THOUGHTS

a world of business that is often driven by shareholder needs, it is very easy to forget the humans working inside organisations. It is worrying enough that many organisations have ignored their business impact on the environment as they focus on satisfying their shareholders. Even more concerning is the fact that many organisations have forgotten about the humans that make them what they are in the first place. An RDHY lens makes you think carefully about your own humanity as a manager and of course the humanity of your fellows, i.e. your employees. Instead of thinking about the bottom line, it is time you began considering the essence of your practice as a manager. Our animal instincts want us to establish who is on top of the food chain, thereby raising winners and losers, Napoleons and commoners, leaders and followers, masters and servants, the strong and the weak, among others. In fact, the entire Darwinian evolutionary idea, in our view, has wrought more harm than good in a world that desperately needs us to be there for one another. Should it be the survival of the fittest or should it be that we grow together as one people, empowered to thrive together and granted autonomy to be who we want to be? You can see why we stand for a new kind of worldview in our practice of management. When you see things differently, you will do things differently. Why should it make the news when Zappos decided to abandon the traditional ideas of hierarchy and manage with holacracy? As humans, we are simply not used to such disruption of 'order'. Zappos did it anyway and they are successful at it, with 82% of its employees saying it is a great place to work in the 2021 Great Place to Work® Global Employee Engagement Survey. Like Zappos' holacracy, RDHY, which also calls for a breaking down of hierarchies, is already making its own news with Haier who have boldly implemented this new philosophy of management in their subsidiaries, including their American acquisition GE Appliances. Indeed, change will attract attention but your commitment to it is what matters.

In RDHY, we see humans (re)organising themselves in ways that make sense as they consider one another as equals, trust one another's abilities and encourage one another to higher levels of achievement. To do so, they believe in the potential of the 'other' and celebrate their 'otherness'. What more can we say? In a world of ubiquitous digital technologies, human relationships can often become what we refer to elsewhere as 'technologised', i.e. social relationships in which technology is as much a part as the humans involved. It therefore takes humans to decide how they reorder themselves with their technology counterparts to make work meaningful. The ball is now in your court. It is time we took a bold step in our practice of management.

Index

360-degree feedback 174
accountability 8, 35, 42, 92
   leadership 154, 159
actor–network theory 54
Adner, Ron 64
advertisements 90
agency 74, 78
agility 35, 38, 40, 43
Ahmadi, Amal 138
Airbnb xvii
algorithms 80, 81
alienated labour 12
Amazon 20
Apple 13, 14, 42, 81, 135, 173
artificial intelligence (AI) 11, 20, 101
   for human resource management (HRM) 18–19
aspirations
   customers 91, 93–4
   employees 114
attention spans 20
automation 10, 39
autonomy 33, 88, 139, 140, 182, 183
   employees xix, 29, 33, 34, 35–6, 65, 114, 128, 133, 179–80, 184, 186

Babbitt, Mark 11
Bain & Company 83
balance 110
Bass, Bernard 122
Baumruk, Ray 103
Bennis, Warren 145
big data 81
blind self (blind spots) 171, 172, 173, 174
blockchain technology 11
Book of Changes (*I Ching*) 110

boundaryless organisation 51, 54, 58, 62, 111–12, 127, 166
brand(s)
   customers emotional connections with 90, 91
   ecosystem 15, 16, 132
   employer 42
   loyalty 85
   platform 15
   product 13, 15
   trust 42
Buchheit, Paul 104
Burns, James MacGregor 122
business
   as ecosystem xxii, 15–21, 22, 33, 34
   world of, in twenty-first century 5–8
business acumen 38
Butler, Timothy 153

capabilities, employee 99–101
capital mobility 6
Carr, Nicholas 20
Carse, James 111
change
   anticipating and responding to 7, 11, 12, 35
   constant 28–9
   cultural barriers to 167
   fear and 138
   openness to 35
   possibility of 140
   and RenDanHeYi (RDHY) model 35, 36–7
   technological 6, 7, 22, 132
charismatic leadership 122
China Building Material Test & Certification Group (CTC) 136
Christensen, Clayton 130

INDEX

Churchill, Winston 11
cloud computing 11
co-creation xvii, 33, 88, 91, 93, 111–13, 114, 126, 137, 191
CoCreate platform 93, 112–13, 114
Coine, Ted 11
collaboration 19, 35, 38, 92, 136, 152, 166, 167, 191
  customer 28, 54, 82, 83, 88, 92–3, 111, 126, 127, 132, 136, 137
  employee 28, 42, 43, 54, 128, 151, 186
  Haier 28, 137, 139–40
  industry–government–education 20–1
  see also co-creation; partnerships
collaborative leadership 137–8
collective value 123
collectivist contexts 166
common good 123, 124, 151
communal element of leadership 169, 171, 172, 174–5
communication 29, 35, 57, 149, 151, 152, 184–5, 191
  with customers 66, 94, 133, 185
compensation, employees *see* reward systems
competencies, managerial 38–40
competition 19, 100–1, 123, 176–7, 191, 192
  for talent 102
computer systems 10–11, 130
Confucianism 110
connected technology architecture 39, 40
connectedness *see* interconnectedness
constant change 28–9
consumerism 7, 92
content wars 19–20
context, understanding your 165–8, 175–7, 190
contingency model of leadership 148
continuous improvement 35

continuous learning 100, 159
contracts
  EMC 108–9, 111–12, 114
  incomplete 111
Cornfield, Gene 64
COVID-19 pandemic 5–6, 7, 17, 41, 91, 127
creativity 28, 33, 34, 35, 65, 100, 106
cultural barriers to change 167
culture, organisational 52, 105–6
customer engagement xx, 16–17, 65–6, 73–96, 180
  collaborative approach to 82, 83, 88
  and customer needs, response to 75–6, 90–1
  emotional connection with brands and 90, 91
  senior leadership and 76–80
  sessions 176
  role of technology in 16, 80–3, 90–1
customer hackathons 66
customer relationship management (CRM) 64, 65
customer satisfaction xxiii, 54
  and employee training programmes 79–80
customer service 34, 36
customer–employee relationship xxii–xxiii, 51–69, 100
  co-creation xi, 33, 88, 91, 93, 111–13, 114, 126, 137, 191
  customer engagement *see* customer engagement
  dangers of not connecting employees and users 64–5
  deepening 129–30, 131
  factors affecting 52–3
  and key performance indicators (KPIs) 57, 58
  organisational structure and 52, 53
  physical engagement 66
  and power 53, 58, 65
  and RenDanHeYi model 53–6, 57–8

and technology 61–3, 67, 114
transactional 52
customer–organisation relationship xxiii, 73–96, 121–2, 132
  customer engagement *see* customer engagement
  and customer member/non-member status 54–5, 58, 74, 92–3
  and customer needs versus wants 75–6, 82
  digital platform interactions 75
  Haier 134–7, 180
  and hierarchical organisations xx, 8, 10
  and senior leadership 76–80, 81–2
  and technology 16, 75, 80–3, 90–1, 93
  zero-distance approach 76, 82
customers (users)
  aspirations 91, 93–4
  as co-creators xvii, 33, 88, 91, 93, 111–13, 114, 126, 137, 191
  collaboration 28, 54, 82, 83, 88, 92–3, 111, 126, 127, 132, 136, 137
  see also co-creation
  communication with 66, 94, 133, 185
  as consumers 130, 131
  data harvesting and analytics 39, 80–1, 83, 84, 90–1
  demographics 94
  disengaged xx–xxi
  distractions for 84–5
  as part of ecosystem micro-communities (EMCs) 57, 58, 73, 85
  empowerment 74
  engagement *see* customer engagement
  experience 15, 17, 74–5, 82, 180
  experience management 81
  feedback 53, 55
  as followers 77–8, 80
  as 'hirer' of product/service 130
  as 'king' 53, 55–6, 79–80
  as leaders 67, 139
  role of leadership in serving 124, 126–7
  loyalty 34, 66, 82, 83, 85–8, 100, 132
  needs 84–5, 88, 90–1, 100, 126, 127, 131, 132, 133, 153, 175–6, 191
  versus wants 75–6, 82
  outside-in perspective of 51, 52–3, 58
  partnership status 88
  power 53, 58, 65, 93
  preferences 84, 85, 93–4, 132
  profiles 91, 93, 132
  as prosumers xvii, 15, 73–4
  in RenDanHeYi (RDHY) model 34, 37, 51, 74, 75–6, 82, 129–30
  reward systems 66, 91
  satisfaction *see* customer satisfaction
  switching 7
  value 32–3, 43, 75–6, 82, 90, 107–8
  values 84
  as watchdogs 7–8

data harvesting and analytics 39, 80–1, 83, 84, 90–1, 154
Davies, Fred 62
Day, George 65
decentralisation xix
decision-making 35, 38, 43, 53, 67, 93, 124
delegation 137–8, 140
demographics 94
design thinking 38, 82
differentiation 14, 20
digital intelligence and modelling 39
digital marketing 84
dignity 88, 133, 183
disintermediation xix
disruptive leadership 38
distant server metaphor xx

distractions, customer 84–5
distributed leadership xix, 126, 149–50, 151
diversity 106, 151, 191
division of labour 8, 53
Drucker, Peter 75

Economic and Philosophical Manuscripts (Marx) 12
ecosystem brands 15, 16, 132
ecosystem era 17, 19, 20, 43, 44, 106, 137, 168
ecosystem micro-communities (EMCs) 51, 53, 57, 67, 89, 92, 105, 128–9, 149
   contracts 109, 111–12, 114
      price war example 108–9
   customers (users) as part of 57, 58, 73, 85
   and leadership 150
   performance measurement 178–82
   see also Haier, ecosystem micro-communities (EMCs)
ecosystem organisation 28–31, 106–7, 123–4
   and constant change principle 28–9
   creativity and innovation in 28
   value creation in 28
ecosystem(s) 13–14
   analysing your 175–7
   businesses as xxii, 15–21, 22, 33, 34
   as a concept xix
education–industry–government collaboration 20–1
Elop, Stephen 173
EMCs *see* ecosystem micro-communities
emotional connection with brands 90, 91
employee engagement xxiii, 99, 103–5, 113–14, 177, 191
   definition of 103
   as human-centric concept 104
employee–organisation relationship xxiii, 55, 99–115

and AI-enabled HRM 18–19
   collaborative 128
   deepening 179–80, 186
   employee engagement *see* employee engagement
   and technology 186
employees
   aspirations 114
   autonomy xix, 29, 33, 34, 35–6, 65, 114, 128, 133, 179–80, 184, 186
   collaboration 28, 42, 43, 54, 128, 139, 151, 186
   compensation *see* reward systems
   empowerment 22, 34, 42, 43, 65, 133, 186, 191
   engagement *see* employee engagement
   entrepreneurial activity 36, 57, 128, 133, 150, 179
   flexible working 114, 177
   hygiene factors 128
   intrapreneurship 57, 107, 128, 149, 151
   as leaders 128, 139, 155, 169
   role of leadership in serving 127–9, 155–6
   loyalty 101
   mobility 101–3, 177, 191
   motivators 128, 129, 151
   needs 128, 129
   organisational pull-factors keeping 102
   as partners 128, 184
   power 127
   as powerhouses of capabilities 99–101
   presenteeism 103
   productivity 128
   psychological safety xxiii, 106, 151
   in RenDanHeYi (RDHY) model 31–3, 34, 35–7, 53–6, 99, 105, 106–8
   as resources 52, 99–100
   reward systems *see* reward systems

INDEX

satisfaction 36–7, 54
self-expression 33, 34, 104
self-hood 103–4
skill sets versus what customers want 56–8
training, and customer satisfaction 79–80
value 180
work–life balance 127, 177
see also customer-employee relationship; employee-organisation relationship
employer brand 42
employment, lifetime 59, 60, 101
empowerment 35
  customers (users) 74
  employee 22, 34, 42, 43, 65, 133, 186, 191
engagement *see* customer engagement; employee engagement
entrepreneurial activity 36, 57, 128, 133, 150, 179
  see also intrapreneurship
entrepreneurial intelligence 38
entrepreneurial leadership 153
The Entrepreneurial Mind (Timmons) 153
environmental performance 154, 155
environmental, social and governance (ESG) framework 154–5, 158
environmental sustainability 39
equality 88, 133
equilibrium 108–9
equity (fairness) 106
Euromonitor International 134

Facebook 13, 14, 77
failure 35, 36, 113
FAST goals 160
fear, and change 138
feedback 186, 191
  360-degree 174
  customer 53, 55
  role model 159

Fiedler, F. 148
The Fifth Discipline (Senge) 160
financial performance 153–5, 158
Finite and Infinite Games (Carse) 111
first industrial revolution 8, 130
FirstBuild 93, 112–13, 114
flat organisational structure 29, 35, 42, 126, 166, 183, 186
flexible working 114, 177
follower-centric leadership models 78, 156, 168, 174
followers, customers as 77–8, 80
Ford, Henry 12
Fortune magazine 77
fourth industrial revolution 6, 11–13, 14, 130
functional specialisation 123

GE Appliances 112, 138, 192, 193
Glassdoor 81
globalisation 6, 92, 154, 157
Gmail 104
goals 52, 105, 128, 140, 153, 178, 192
  FAST 160
  shared 64, 124, 127, 149
  SMART 160
  stretch 158–9
Google 81, 104
Google Currents 63
governance 154
government
  collaboration with universities/industry 20–1
  policy 176
Grand View Research 81
'great man' theory of leadership 121, 152
Greenleaf, Robert 146, 149
Grint, Keith 146, 152–3
growth 153, 154
  sustainable 132–7
Gudala, Sudhakar 90

199

INDEX

hackathons, customer 66
Haier xxii, 15–16, 21, 27–31, 33, 34, 37, 41, 44, 57, 79, 83, 92, 138, 150–1, 189, 192, 193
   air conditioner (AC) industry 134–7, 138
   collaboration 28, 137, 139–40
   customer–organisation relationship 134–7, 180
   ecosystem micro-communities (EMCs) 29–31, 85–8, 90, 107–8, 109, 112, 128, 132–3, 155
   node microenterprises 133
   performance measurement 179–80
   shared services platform 133
   Smart Cooking EMC 86–7
   Smart Kitchen EMC 29, 31
   Smart Laundry EMC 90
   user microenterprises 133
   employee autonomy 179–80
   employee leadership 128
   entrepreneurial mindset 179
   flat organisational structure 19, 35
   innovation focus 27, 28
   Internet of Air 134–5, 155, 192
   Internet of Food (IoF) EMC 86–7, 88, 107–8, 123, 132, 192
   Internet of Things (IoT) 132–3
   Internet of Water 192
   partnership approach to development 135–6, 137
   research and development (R&D) 135–6
   Sanyo acquisition 58–61, 150, 151
   shared organisational spaces 126
   sustainable business growth 132–7
   turnover and profit 33
Haier Biomedical 107
Haier Germany 91
Hakkarainen, Ari 173
Hart, Oliver 111
Harvard Business Review 153
Hauser, John 90

Healthy Air Ecosystem Alliance 136
Herzberg, Frederick 128
Hesse, Hermann 146, 147, 156
hidden self 171, 172
hierarchical organisational structure xx, 6–7, 28, 53
   challenges for 8–15
   customers and xx, 8, 10
hiring policy 57, 106
Hollywood 19–20
Holmstrom, Bent 111
honesty 170
Honeywell 135
human resource management (HRM) 56–7
   AI-enabled 18–19
human-centricity 33, 39, 44, 62, 75, 76, 80, 82, 83, 104, 107, 109, 114, 123, 129, 137–8, 174, 192–4
human–technology relationship 61–2
humility 110, 139
hybrid working 7, 114, 151
hygiene factors 128

I Ching 110
IDEO 82
IKEA 73
improvement, continuous 35
inclusion 106
incomplete contracts 111
individualistic contexts 166
Industrial Age 12
industrial revolutions
   first 8, 130
   fourth 6, 11–13, 14, 131
   second 8, 130
   third 10–11, 130
industry analysis 19
industry–government–education collaboration 20–1
influence
   leadership 122, 156, 191
   multidirectional 126

informating 10
information and communication
	technology (ICT) 10, 92, 132
information management
	systems 65
Ingham, Harrington 170
innovation 35, 42, 100, 106
	and ecosystem organisation 28
	Haier focus on 27, 28
	and hierarchical organisation 28
	open 28
	product 35, 100, 150
inter-organisational teams 151
interconnectedness xix, xxi, 15, 41–2,
	43, 110–11, 122–4, 126–7, 131
	leadership and 145, 149–51, 156–8
	spatial/geographic 148–9
interdependence 124, 128
International Data Corporation
	(IDC) 81
Internet 149
	mobile 13
Internet of Air 134–5, 155, 192
Internet of Food (IoF) 86–7, 88,
	107–8, 123, 132, 192
Internet of Things (IoT) xix, 11, 20, 67,
	85, 92, 107, 111, 131, 132–3,
	192
Internet of Water 192
intrapreneurship 57, 107, 128,
	149, 151
iPhone 13
iTunes 13

Johari window 160, 170–2, 174, 186
A Journey to the East (Hesse) 146, 147

Kahn, William 103, 104
Kaplan, R S. 154
Kaplan, Sarah 152
key performance indicators (KPIs)
	57, 58
knowledge sharing 35

labour
	alienated 12
	brawn and brain perspectives of
		99–100
	division of 8, 53
labour market 6
	dynamism 101
	external 101
	internal 101
Laker, B. 159
Latour, Bruno 54
Law, John 55
'leader servant' 147
Leaders Eat Last (Sinek) 147
leadership xxiii–xxiv, 43, 117–29,
	137–9, 190
	accountability 159
	boss-centred 148
	charismatic 122
	collaborative 137–8
	communal element of 169, 171,
		172, 174–5
	contextual element of 169, 175–7
	contingency model of 148
	customers (users) 67, 139
	definitions of 121, 145–6
	disruptive 38
	distributed xix, 126, 149–50, 151
	and ecosystem micro-communities
		(EMCs) 150
	employees 128, 139, 155, 169
	entrepreneurial 153
	follower-centric 78, 156, 168, 174
	'great man' theory of 121, 152
	influence 122, 156, 191
	for an interconnected ecosystem
		145, 149–51, 156–8
	as multidirectional 122–3
	personal element of 169–75
	personal transformation and
		121–3
	and power 147, 148
	project 39

201

leadership xxiii–xxiv (*continued*)
   and RenDanHeYi (RDHY)
      model 121–2, 126–7, 137–9,
      150–1, 155
   resilience in 152–3
   roadmap for development 158–9
   role models 159
   role in serving the customer 124, 126–7
   role in serving employees 127–9, 155–6
   self- 169–75
   senior, and customer–organisation relationship 76–80, 81–2
   servant xxiii, 145–8, 149, 155–7
   service 156, 166
   shared xix, 126
   situational 126, 148
   style 159–60
   subordinate-centred 148
   trait approach to 121, 122, 124, 126, 152–3
   transactional 122
   transformational 122
learning, continuous 100, 159
lifetime employment 59, 60, 101
Liu Zhanjie 107
loyalty
   brand 85
   customers (users) 34, 66, 82, 83, 85–8, 100, 132
   employees 101
Luft, Joseph 170

Maklan, Stan 64
Malik, Ashish 18
marketing, digital 84
Marketing Metrics 83
Marx, Karl 12
mass production 8, 12–13
matrix organisational structure 151, 183
McMillan, D. 154

mechanised production 8, 130
Mella mushroom-growing appliance 113
mentoring relationships 156, 160
Microsoft 173
Mintzberg, Henry 129, 169, 175
Mitchell, Jack 79
Mitsubishi Electric 135
mixed/extended reality (XR) 11
mobile Internet 13
mobile phones *see* smartphones
mobility
   capital 6
   employees 101–3, 177, 191
Moore, James F. 111
motivators, employee 128, 129, 151
Motorola, Moto Maker 74
Musk, Elon 76–7

Nanus, Burt 145
Nash equilibrium 108–9
needs
   employees 128, 129
   technology 168
   see also customers (users), needs
Negm, Walid 14
Netflix 14, 20
network-enabled business model 17, 18
networks xvii, xix, 13, 15, 17, 22, 33, 54, 123, 133, 150, 167, 175
Nightingale, Florence 146
Nike 13
node microenterprises 133
Nokia 173

Ogilvy, David 79
open innovation 28
open plan offices 11
open self 171–2
OpenIDEO 82
openness 34, 38, 127, 135, 137, 139–40, 150

organisation–customer relationship
see customer–organisation
relationship
organisation–employee relationship
see employee–organisation
relationship
organisational culture 52, 105–6
organisational resilience 152, 153,
155
organisational structure 183, 186
and customer–employee
relationship 52, 53
matrix 151, 183
see also flat organisational structure;
hierarchical organisational
structure
organisational values 76, 105–6,
183, 192
Ouchi, William 101

Parsons, Talcott 53
participating technologies 16–17,
18, 20, 37, 39, 62, 77, 130–1,
137
partnerships 149
customer 88
employee 128, 184
Haier 135–6, 137
see also collaboration
Pereira, Vijay 37–8, 40
performance 149, 158
assessing, measuring and improving
178–82
environmental, social and
governance (ESG) dimensions
of 154–5, 158
financial 153–5, 158
performance-based reward systems
32–3, 60, 61, 184
personalisation 15
Pharmacy Unscripted® 63
platform brands 15–16
platform economy xvii–xviii, 13, 19

'Ponzi' schemes 78
Porter, Michael 19
power
customer (user) 53, 58, 65, 93
and customer–employee relationship
53, 58, 65
devolution of (shared) 139,
140, 166
employees 127
formal and informal 53
and leadership 147, 148
multidirectional 126
power distance 139, 166
preferences, customers 84, 85,
93–4, 132
presenteeism 103
price wars 108–9
problem-solving 38
process innovation 35
product brands 13, 15
product design and development 82,
93, 132, 134–7, 150
product innovation 35, 100, 150
product-based business model
17–18
productivity 128
profit 34, 192
sharing 32–3
progress, sharing stories of 185,
191–2
project leadership 39
prosumers xvii, 15, 73–4
psychological safety xxiii, 106, 151

quantum management 110

'rainforest' businesses 33, 34, 139
reflection, skill of 170
reflexivity 170
regulatory environment 176
relevance 14
remote working 7
remuneration see reward systems

INDEX

RenDanHeYi (RDHY) model xxi–xxii, xxiii, 1, 21, 27, 31–3, 44, 150–1
  assessing readiness for implementing 178, 181–2
  and change 35, 36–7
  competencies as opportunities for personal growth in 38–40
  continuous improvement and 35
  customer-centricity 34, 37, 51, 74, 75–6, 82, 129–30
  and customer–employee relationship 53–6, 57–8
  and employees 31–3, 34, 35–7, 53–6, 99, 105, 106–8
  entrepreneurial mindset 36, 57
  and leadership 121–2, 126–7, 137–9, 150–1, 155
  opportunities and benefits of adopting 37–43
  and performance 149
  reward system 32–3, 60, 61
  talent management 35–6
  and technology 61–3
  value creation 32–3, 181–2
  value matrix 181–2
RenDanheYi (RDHY) triad 27, 32, 44
research and development (R&D), Haier 135–6
research institutions 20–1, 135–6
research orientation 39
resilience
  individual 152
  in leadership 152–3
  organisational 152, 153, 155
resource-based perspective 19
resources, employees as 52, 99–100
reverse mentoring 156
reward systems 52, 102, 150, 151, 184
  customer 66, 91
  performance-based 32–3, 60, 61, 184
  RenDanHeYi (RDHY) model 32–3, 60, 61
  seniority-based 32, 59, 60

risk mitigation 42
risk-taking 22, 35
robotics 11, 39
Rodriguez, Bernardo 74–5
role models 159
Ross, J. W. 90–1
Rost, Joseph 78

Samsung 42, 173
Sanyo 138
  Haier acquisition of 58–61, 150, 151
SAP 17
Sasser, W. Earl 83
satisfaction *see* customer satisfaction; employees, satisfaction
Schmidt, W. H. 148
Schumpeter, Joseph 10
second industrial revolution 8
security, technology 42, 63, 91, 130
self
  blind (blind spots) 171, 172, 173, 174
  hidden 171, 172
  open 171–2
  unknown 171, 172, 174
self-expression 33, 34, 104, 113
self-hood, employees 103–4
self-leadership 169–75
self-organising teams 43
Selfridge, Harry 79
Senge, peter 160
seniority-based systems 32, 59, 60, 101, 150
servant leadership xxiii, 145–8, 149, 155–7
service leadership 156, 166
service philosophy 65
Shanghai Hitachi 135
shared cognition xxiii, 99, 105, 123
shared goals 64, 124, 127, 149
shared knowledge 35
shared leadership xix, 126
shared organisational spaces 126

shared power 139, 140, 166
shared services platforms 133
shared value systems 33, 64, 66, 109, 123, 124
shared values 105, 183
shareholder value 34, 180
sharing economy xvii
silo mentality 110, 123
Simzer, Kevin 41–2
Sinek, Simon 76, 147
situational leadership 126, 148
SMART goals 160
smartphones 131, 173
social concerns 154, 155
social media xx, 11, 20, 84, 90, 94, 114, 132, 140, 148–9
  see also Facebook; Twitter
social movements 8
social values 85
Soga, Lebene 138
Srivatsa, Anand 43
Stodgill, Ralph 121
strengths, recognising 166–7
stretch goals 158–9
structure, organisational *see* organisational structure
success, sharing stories of 185
suppliers 175, 176, 185
sustainability, environmental/social 39, 155
sustainable business growth 132–7
SWOT analysis 19

talent
  competition for 102
  management 35–6
  marketplace 101–3
  supply and demand 102
Tanenbaum, R 148
Tansley, Arthur 15
Taoist thinking 110
teams
  autonomy within 36

  collaboration and cooperation within 42
  empowerment 22
  inter-organisational 151
  self-organising 43
  trust 36
technological change 6, 7, 22, 132
technology 140, 141, 154, 184, 190
  'admin rights' 63
  back-up plan 168
  bespoke 63
  and customer–employee relationship 61–3, 67, 114
  and customer–organisation relationship 16, 75, 80–3, 90–1, 93
  and employee–organisation relationship 186
  and interconnectedness 148–9
  needs 168
  security 42, 63, 91, 130
  updates 63
  user-friendly 62, 63
  see also information and communication technology; participating technologies
Tesla 76–7
Theory Z 101
Theresa, Mother 146
third industrial revolution 10–11, 130
Thomke, Stefan 90
TikTok 20
Timmons, Jeffrey 153
Timoshenko 90
Tirrell, Matthew 20–1
Toffler, Alvin xvii, 15, 73–4
Tomlinson, B. 154
Training Magazine 79
training programmes, and customer satisfaction 79–80
trait approach to leadership 121, 122, 124, 126, 152–3
transactional leadership 122

205

transformational leadership 122
Trump, Donald 77
trust 34, 36, 42
   brand 42
Twitter 76–7, 78

Uber xvii, 13, 14
uniqueness 14
universities 20–1
unknown self 171, 172, 174
user microenterprises 133
users *see* customers (users)

value
   collective 123
   creation 28, 32–3, 43, 75–6, 82, 90, 107–8, 180, 181–2, 185
   employee 180
   shareholder 34, 180
   sharing 33, 64, 66, 109, 123, 124, 185
values
   customers 84
   organisational 76, 105–6, 183, 192
   shared 105, 183
   social 85

virtual reality (VR) 11
vision-casting 140
VUCA (volatility, uncertainty, complexity and ambiguity) 19, 148

Walgreens Boots Alliance 63
'walled garden' businesses 33–4
weaknesses, recognising 167
Weather China 136
Web 3.0 11
Weber, Max 12
work–life balance 127, 177
A World Gone Social (Coine and Babbitt) 11

Xiaomi 40, 41

Yukl, Gary 106, 191

Zappos 193
Zhang Ruimin 21, 27, 139, 166, 189
Zohar, Danah 110
Zuboff, Shoshana 10